Whispers *in the* Wheatfield

Finding Inspiration and Purpose
in the Wrinkles of Everyday Living

Whispers *in the* Wheatfield

Finding Inspiration and Purpose
in the Wrinkles of Everyday Living

Joseph M. Korzon

Copyright © 2025 Joseph M. Korzon. All rights reserved.

No part of this publication may be reproduced, stored in a retrieval system or transmitted in any form or by any means, electronic, mechanical, photocopying, recording or otherwise, without prior permission of Halo Publishing International.

The views and opinions expressed in this book are those of the author and do not necessarily reflect the official policy or position of Halo Publishing International. Any content provided by our authors are of their opinion and are not intended to malign any religion, ethnic group, club, organization, company, individual or anyone or anything.

Some of the images within this book were generated using artificial intelligence technology.

For permission requests, write to the publisher, addressed "Attention: Permissions Coordinator," at the address below.

Halo Publishing International
7550 W IH-10 #800, PMB 2069,
San Antonio, TX 78229

First Edition, August 2025
ISBN: 978-1-63765-800-0
Library of Congress Control Number: 2025911514

The information contained within this book is strictly for informational purposes. Unless otherwise indicated, all the names, characters, businesses, places, events and incidents in this book are either the product of the author's imagination or used in a fictitious manner. Any resemblance to actual persons, living or dead, or actual events is purely coincidental.

Halo Publishing International is a self-publishing company that publishes adult fiction and non-fiction, children's literature, self-help, spiritual, and faith-based books. We continually strive to help authors reach their publishing goals and provide many different services that help them do so. We do not publish books that are deemed to be politically, religiously, or socially disrespectful, or books that are sexually provocative, including erotica. Halo reserves the right to refuse publication of any manuscript if it is deemed not to be in line with our principles. Do you have a book idea you would like us to consider publishing? Please visit www.halopublishing.com for more information.

This book is dedicated to family and friends, old and new, who have offered me inspiration, guidance, and encouragement over many years. It is with humility and appreciation that I dedicate this book to them and to all who have shown the courage and commitment of friendship, service, and love to those in need!

An Invitation

In this literary anthology and journey, the author invites us to explore the intricacies and surprises of daily life through a tapestry of short stories, essays, and observations, many coming from the author's rich collection of life experiences, all of which invite each of us to navigate our way through the vastness of life and all of its unpredictability, unveiling the whispers of inspiration and profound purpose that are often hidden in the most ordinary moments of our life journey.

While part of our journey may be filled with turbulence and numerous challenges, these can serve as catalysts that lead us to profound insights into life and inspire us to discover our formula and pathway to living successfully and finding joy and peace along the way.

This book is intended to inspire others to explore the full range of emotions, memories, and reflections within their own lives and to discover the beauty and wisdom that emerge from the complexities and fullness of everyday living.

Contents

An Invitation	9
Whispers of Insight: An Introduction	17
Run with the Wind, Cry in the Rain	27
Fruitful Thanksgiving	35
The Book of James (For Grandson James)	39
A Brotherhood Beneath the Elms	43
Happy Hour at Njoki's	49
Time and Tide	61
Dreamer's Soliloquy	65
New Awakening	67
Glowing Embers	69
Starry Night	73
Still Waters	77
Crab on a Leash	81
A Celebration of Light	87
Peaceful Hearts	91
Benevolent Messenger: To My Guardian Angel	95

To My Guardian Angel	95
Sweet Discovery: Lily and Rose	99
Outlook on Life	103
Rainy-Day Malaise	107
Olde Wood	111
Olde Wood	115
Where the Sweet: Spirits Dwell	117
Pivot Point	123
The Book of Chaos	127
Another Brick in the Wall	131
Silent Passage	135
Note to Self	139
Winter Upon Us	143
Courage…to Love	147
Today, Be Gone!	151
Imperfect Practice	155
For the Love of Jessie: A Desert Love Story	159
A Calling of Echoes	169
Into the Sublime	173
Nate's Way	175
A Field of Dreams	177
The Circle Game	183
A Matter of Perspective	187

Calls to the Heart	191
Find Your Way: Whisper's Poem	193
Reflections	195
Poor Me! A Thanksgiving Day Lament	199
Autumn's Embrace	203
In the Nick of Time	207
Fear, Uncertainty, and Doubt: Part 1—The Call	211
Fear, Uncertainty, and Doubt: Part 2—The Hope	215
Summer Awakening	219
Risk Management	221
Compelling Transition	223
On the Right Path	227
Fatal Vision	231
Absolute Zeros	233
Strokes of Genius	237
Connected Starlight	239
Point of View	243
Culpable Hearts	247
Thorn and Seed	251
The Right Spin	253
Synchronicity of Hearts	257
In the Storm	261
Spanish String Theory	265

A Cut Above: Between the Rainbows	269
Measure Up	275
Unhurried Blessings	279
Empty Glass	283
In the Shadow of Our Conscience	287
A Concinnated Calling	291
A Christmas Wish	295
Breakfast in a Parallel Universe	299
Cold Calculations	307
Sweet Arrival: Mitch's Way	311
Wonder of Night	315
Eye of the Beholder	319
Mindful Dissonance	325
Reflecting Pool	329
Progressive Assurance	333
Arrogant Ambivalence	337
Paternal Exuberance	341
Bright Idea	345
Slice of Time	349
Time Sensitive	353
Number the Heroes	357
Empathetic Awakenings	361
First Day of Forever	365

First Rule of Holes	369
Awaken, Oh Peaceful Heart	375
Shifting Sands	377
Addictive Personality: For Ed	381
Altered States	385
As Kindness Does (For Cece)	389
Forgotten Moments	391
Back to the Garden	393
Secret Place	395
About Being Authentic	397
Illumination	401
Renews the Heart	405
Guiding Light	409
Tender Moment	411
Uncertain Reality: A Matter of Quantum Spirituality	417
Cosmic Threads: Connecting in an Infinite Universe	423
Reality Check: Cultural Realism and Ultimate Truth	427
Brown-Eyed Girl	431
A Pathway Home	445
About the Author	**447**

Whispers of Insight

An Introduction

It has been said that intuition is the diligent messenger of the spirit. When I first began compiling my thoughts into a collection of writings for this book, I thought that *Whispers* would be my attempt to provide others with guidance on how best to live a successful life. It was a noble thought, but ill-timed at best and very naïve. But let us set aside naiveté for the moment; I was young, arrogant, and most ignorant about life and everything related to it, but I did have a vision.

In my mind's eye, I saw a giant wheatfield stretching as far as I could see out to the horizon. Cut into that endless vision of tall brown shafts were pathways, rivers of wind, winding their way through the stretches of wheat, bending the tall shafts, and revealing direction. I saw that endless field of wheat and the pathways cut by the wind as symbolic of my life journey and the inspirations, or insights, I had experienced that helped me decide which path to follow as I made my way down the road of life.

As I grew older and compiled more of life's richness and regrets, I came to understand that the directions or pathways to follow while on one's journey might be revealed in vastly different ways. At times, the direction is as obvious as the swath left by a tempest as it rips its way through the field and bends the tall plants to the breaking point as they lean forward with clear direction. At other times, we must stand quietly and strain our eyes, using all our senses to catch a whisper of inspiration; the tall shafts flutter in the breeze and quietly point our way forward.

Years have passed since my vision, and I have learned that inspiration comes to those who are open to it. However, receiving inspiration does not guarantee following the right path—free will always prevails over divine guidance.

That is why it is so necessary for us to stay connected to the spirit within us. The better connected we are, the better the chances are that we will see and follow the right path for us in our lives as we move forward towards our destiny.

Through numerous experiences of failure, disappointment, success, and reconciliation, I have come to understand that although we share a common destiny, the path we choose towards that destiny significantly influences the amount of joy, peace, and love we experience along the way. This observation, while seemingly evident, is important enough to warrant a reminder.

My journey has included experiences that have bounced me between heaven and hell, with ample time spent in the highs and lows of life. I learned at an early age about the feelings of loss, thanks to both of my parents—one parent through an early death, and the other parent through emotional unavailability because of that death.

As if that were not enough for a young teenager, I had to deal with the alcoholism of my older brother, who had come home from military service on a hardship discharge after my father became ill. The term "hardship discharge" seemed quite appropriate, as I learned quickly just how much of a hardship his discharge would bring to all of us as his alcoholism raged. Years later, that same brother would go on to defeat his alcoholism, committing himself to sobriety and to helping many others beat those same demons. I came to admire him and his strength before he died from dementia over forty years later.

As an older teen, I took a nontraditional approach to education. With help and encouragement from LSD advocate Dr. Timothy Leary, I found a temporary escape from the painful reality of my home life by fitting the occasional acid trip and transcendental meditation techniques of Maharishi Mahesh Yogi into a sustainable avoidance of emotional and social maturity, temporarily lightening the load of my responsibilities at home.

Through those years of self-imposed turbulence, I am sure that my guardian angel, though tested to the point of resignation, watched over me in horror, but also with a determination to guide my steps one at a time, helping me to find solid ground for my feet and acceptance in the hearts of others who would provide the comfort, love, and encouragement around which my psyche could rally and rebuild. The help I needed at that moment came in the form of a beautiful college undergrad, another guardian angel perhaps, who somehow perceived in me the seeds of greatness sown by our Creator but hidden beneath the rubble and turbulence that was my persona when we first met.

Meeting this blonde, blue-eyed coed from a normal and supportive family was a lifesaving experience for me. Not only did her presence help to turn me away from the destructive behaviors that I used to numb the pain of my floundering climb into adulthood, but as an adult, I also experienced love and being in love for the very first time in my life. During those years of calm and commitment, I reveled in the joy of the moment. I also began to reacquaint myself with the Lord and refocus on my spirituality.

From that point forward, my life grew exponentially. Marriage, a real career, returning to college in the evenings, and fatherhood were all welcome experiences as I grew in confidence about my business success and broadened that definition to include my family, friendships, and a growing sense of responsibility to help others. The latter would prove to be a double-edged sword, turning my passion for helping others into fulfilling the desires of a young man whose adolescent life had been voided by the weight of responsibility for an ill father, a depressed mother, an abusive sibling, and a self-destructive lifestyle. Nevertheless, my instability aside, this period in my life yielded lasting friendships as well as two wonderful sons and two beautiful grandsons.

A divorce and a job loss—to be followed later in my life by other failed relationships and other job losses—would open old wounds and create new challenges for me as I struggled to find a new center point to help me rebalance my life and find within myself a better understanding of who I was and what purpose or meaning was attached to my existence.

During those difficult years, my guardian angel was doing its best to guide me forward in my growth, but there is a limit to how much guidance and inspiration an individual can receive as a whisper in a wheatfield. My life needed something greater, something more impactful and undeniable.

That impact came in the form of a phone call in the early hours of one steamy August night when I got the news that my nineteen-year-old son had been critically injured in an automobile accident. Life signaled that a different person was needed to meet the new challenges.

Over the months and years following my son's accident, I would develop an acute awareness and knowledge of those things related to traumatic brain injury, emergency surgeries, rehabilitation hospitals, medications, etc. It was the education that I never had or wanted. But in time, the devastation and chaos of that accident, along with all that followed, gave way to a new realization of personal strength, resilience, and answered prayers. Sadly, these would all be put to the test once again some years later with the accidental death of a friend's twenty-nine-year-old son.

Life moved on for me, as did my career, with the continued ups and downs that seemed to be the pattern of my work life. At times, I would allow myself to feel unlucky. It wasn't fun. I wasn't getting any younger either, which began to weigh on me as I grew anxious about having enough resources to sustain me later in my life. I had learned a great deal from my experiences over the past thirty years. I felt more secure and confident in my strengths and capabilities. I was better prepared for whatever life threw at me, but I still struggled with my purpose and meaning.

One day, when I was between jobs, I was sitting on my sofa, sipping my morning coffee and thinking about what I needed to do that day. I struggled with uncertainty and frustration over the slow process of job interviews, updating resumes, and other tasks. I stopped momentarily to question whether the position I was applying for was right for me. I thought about the same trade-offs that I had struggled with during the other periods of uncertainty in my life—the need for income, job satisfaction, and my overall lack of happiness. Despite all that I had experienced over the previous years, including tragedies, failures, challenges, and successes, I still had not learned that happiness isn't something to be compromised, nor an externally dependent quality of living. What was I missing?

In that moment of frustration and reflection, I realized that the happiness and purpose for which I was searching were both different edges of the same blade. I also learned that I had tried to bully life into accepting my ideas of success and purpose; I was trying to steer a river rather than navigate it. In that moment of complete resignation, I turned over control of my life journey to a higher power, asking out loud, "Lord, tell me what job you want me to do, and I will do it!"

In the silence of that moment, somewhere between my heart and mind, I heard a clear and firm voice say, "Your job is to shine for me!" I immediately understood what that meant and what I needed to focus on. This time, the inspiration came as a whisper, but its impact was as significant as any I had experienced in life up to that point—or even up to the present, for that matter.

In the years that followed, I was able to make up for much of the time I lost early in my career and my personal life. The right opportunities seemed to show up unexpectedly. I excelled in my new job, regaining financial stability and spiritual well-being. In those later years, I even had the opportunity to travel to many parts of the world and experience diverse cultures, forming new friendships and gaining valuable insights into living along the way. I even met another guardian angel, an Irish step-dancing one, and a kindred spirit, thereby extending my circle of family and friends, and capturing another grandson in the process.

While challenges still arise and I still feel anxious at times, allowing myself to give in to that emotion, I no longer need to question myself about the meaning of my life or the purpose of my existence. Simply, it is to bring praise and glory to the one who placed me here on this twisting stone and set me afloat on the river of life, and to love myself and all with whom I share this twisting stone unconditionally.

I now realize that sharing my life experiences and my moments of inspiration is a way to help others find within themselves the echoes of their victories and the inspiration they need to find the opportunity and humility to live out their lives in happiness and in the faith that for them, as it is for me, the best is yet to be.

Run with the Wind, Cry in the Rain

An undeniable truism of our existence is that life is unfair. People don't always get what they deserve. Often, we experience life through a lens of disappointment, unfulfilled dreams, and reflections of things that have gone wrong. We adjust; we move forward.

But nothing could have prepared me for that summer day many years ago when my world changed with a phone call late on a sultry August evening. In the blink of an eye, the unforgiving and inescapable laws of physics, mixed with youthful exuberance, speed, and alcohol, changed my world forever. Traumatic brain injury, vegetative state, coma simulation, rehabilitation, case management—all became part of a strange and unfamiliar vocabulary and an unwanted reality.

In an instant, my son's college plans, our family trips, our sports dialogue, and discussions about career choices and summer concerts gave way to a silence that would not yield for what seemed like an eternity. All that was left was to deal with this new reality of hopes, fears, and feelings of betrayal. Why *our* family?

Earlier that summer, I had worked up to an aggressive series of long runs, cross-training routines, and strengthening programs, all targeted to prepare myself for my goal—running the Boston Marathon the following April. I ran my first marathon in October and finished the race in a respectable time, but I still needed to shave off another thirty-five minutes to qualify for Boston. I trained hard and ran twenty miles and more in practice at a qualifying pace, so I was optimistic about reaching my goal.

But, now, a new reality. Upon opening the door to the ICU, I am bombarded with the chirps, clicks, beeps, and pings of the devices tethering my boy to this side of forever. A glance from the ICU nurse, careful not to make direct eye contact with me, a passing whisper of "he's holding his own." I sit by his bed, careful not to tangle the plumbing that keeps him breathing, and I wait, and I pray.

The day passes like an encroaching fog as I see the lights go on in the parking lot below. It's time to leave. I head to my home and break open a couple of light beers, sit on the sofa in the family room, and turn on the TV, with no care about what program is on, but eager for the bright light and background sound as I sit quietly in the eerie shadows cast by the muted TV. My thoughts bounce between the issues from that day, my younger son just starting his freshman year in high school and not having the full attention of both parents at such a critical time in his life, and what life will be like for me going forward.

I was always conscious that the phone could ring at any moment with an ominous update or worse. I needed to keep my wits about me; I needed to be responsible. I needed to be a father and advocate. I held the phone on my chest and tried to fall asleep, even if just for an hour or so. Each time I awoke, I checked my phone to ensure it was working correctly and I hadn't missed any calls.

The days turned into weeks and the weeks into months. Things had stabilized at the hospital, but were still far from normal. Decisions needed to be made about the next steps. It was clear that I needed to turn my attention towards rehabilitation, but there were so many questions, issues, and alternatives to consider. I had been at the hospital every day for months on end. Now I had to face the prospect of moving my son to a new facility nearly two hours away, with new caretakers and new surroundings, less access for my visits, and more opportunities for the demons to haunt me.

However, as with all change, once you accept it, you find a way to use it to your advantage. The move to a more distant rehabilitation facility provided me with an opportunity to take back a little bit of my life. I started working again and began to socialize. During that socialization, I began to discuss what I had experienced over the previous months. It felt good, although it may not have always been comfortable for those upon whose ears my story fell.

I started getting back into some of my old routines—dinner with a friend, a movie, and even a holiday party if I dared. Along with the socializing, I began to think again about running and my hard work trying to qualify for the

Boston Marathon, all of which had come to an unexpected and debilitating halt with the August phone call. So I set my sights on recapturing the fitness and preparedness I had achieved before my life took an unexpected turn.

The weather was turning colder. The warm days began giving way to grey skies, leafless trees, and windy days, with a fair warning of what was to follow. While I fought off the occasional demons as the evenings lengthened, I was also beginning to feel the need to fully right myself by lacing up my running shoes and stepping back onto the familiar streets.

When I could no longer hold back the desire to capture some of what I had come to know and love in my morning runs, I prepared again in a familiar ritual of dressing, lacing, adjusting, and stretching. Out the door I went into the street. It was a windy November day, and light rain was falling. I could see my breath in the air before I began my run. It was morning, quiet, and I began to experience a familiar peace I had sorely missed.

I flipped down my hood and started putting one foot down and then another, picking up the pace as I neared a quiet Main Street. As my breathing became more pronounced and filled the air in front of me, I could feel the rhythm of my pace becoming more regular. Finally, I was experiencing a savored moment in a familiar environment. It felt wonderful.

As I approached a familiar turn on my route, I could also sense the wind shifting behind me. As I made the turn, the rain intensified. I could feel the rain landing hard on my face and the wind behind me like a hand on the middle of my back. Without warning, the weight of the past several months came upon me with such gravity and suddenness that I was caught entirely off guard.

My breath became irregular, my hands and legs began to tremble, and my face contorted. My mouth opened wide, and I cried out in some odd utterance of both pain and joy, my tears mixing with the cold rain. I no longer felt the need to hide my tears or pretend. All that was left was pure release and acknowledgment of the new reality—one life had been spared; many other lives would be forever changed. It was time to welcome the new person among us and to move forward with realistic possibilities for him and all of us.

That day, I finished my run knowing there would be other days for me to be responsible, to be a father, and to manage the madness. Although uncertain days lay ahead, there would be different races and challenges to focus on and more opportunities to feel the wind at my back and cry in the rain.

Author's note: August 3, 2026, marks the thirtieth anniversary of my eldest son's automobile accident. Over these years, we have been fortunate to have him with us, sharing his humor, mischievous smile, and undeniable personality. He has experienced a life that few thought possible early in his treatment and recovery. We have all witnessed the compassion and dedication of the healthcare and assisted-living professionals who have supported my son over these years, even surviving a COVID-19 hospitalization in 2020.

Now, sipping my morning coffee in my Ellington, Connecticut, home, I often reflect on all that has happened since that August evening many years ago, and I am filled with a great sense of thanksgiving and insight for the miracle that sustained faith has provided us. It has amplified the feelings of brotherhood, connection, and love for each other; amplified that we are all unique threads in the quilt of humankind, and that whatever each one of us does or experiences inevitably tugs and influences the rest of us.

Though I never did end up running the Boston Marathon, I ran the Aetna Hartford Marathon in October of the following year, again finishing in four hours and nine minutes.

Fruitful Thanksgiving

Growing up in the shadows of Yale Bowl meant experiencing the holidays in special ways. For me, this was especially true when it came to Thanksgiving.

The calling of football, family visits, and endless food has always made Thanksgiving an irresistible combination of sights, sounds, and tastes to be savored on that special day, and then again as part of a wonderful string of memories, as if they were shiny gems put away for safekeeping, to be opened again and appreciated the following year. For many of us, having had the benefit of experiencing many of these special moments as a part of a long and interesting life, we can find ourselves occasionally tangled in yesterday's memories as we plan for the new holiday season.

We rise from our comfortable sleep and step into the firm reality of the waiting day. We struggle temporarily to gain clarity of vision as we make our way towards a mixture of swirling milk and caffeine, gathering our complete vision and thoughts into a homogeneous blend that both soothes and prepares us for whatever life presents us with this day. It is a new dawn, a present to be opened, another day to be lived, another chance to be, to love, and to serve.

Each morning, when we have the privilege of greeting the rising sun and reaching the beginnings of a new day, we are instantly confronted with choices about how to spend our daily allotment of precious minutes. Our minds are instantly filled with the remnants of yesterday's successes and failures as we begin to weave together a pattern for the next twenty-four hours of living.

Before we have sipped our way into a full awakening, we are bombarded with information and updates about the world around us, about our loved ones, and about those life issues that seem so impactful on our peace of mind and on our enjoyment of the day ahead.

We hear the words about the lack of kindness and sensitivity in the world, about the failure to put another's interests before our own and to view our day and destiny as something shared and integral to the welfare and well-being of others. We struggle to understand the expectations set upon us to improve our condition, as well as that of the countless faces we will encounter as we journey through our day.

We look for answers from all directions, and between the disturbing lines we read each morning, we search for the right words to express our disappointment in our failures and for a way to renew our commitment to being better today than we were yesterday. We stir our coffee again to awaken it. We remind ourselves in the process that the words that we are searching for wait patiently between our sighs and echo softly within the language of our hearts.

While we may linger briefly on the memories of the bitter fruits we have encountered on our journey, we wrap ourselves in the familiarity of those emotions that have fallen softly upon our hearts. Silently, we move our minds and attention down our list of aspirations and desired behaviors, taking note of those things we have accomplished and those still awaiting our full embrace.

Joy, peace, patience, kindness, goodness, faithfulness, gentleness, self-control, and love—these are the Fruits of the Spirit upon which we feed our souls and with which we transform our minds. Each is a step towards our rightful living and evidence of our progress towards our shared destiny. Each is a reminder of our unique place in creation and of the collective consciousness that we share.

So as we begin to unwrap the gift of today that has been prepared for us, let us reach out to those around us and those within us in appreciation for the opportunity of the new holiday, never taking for granted the brevity of life or our ability to make better the lives of those with whom we journey.

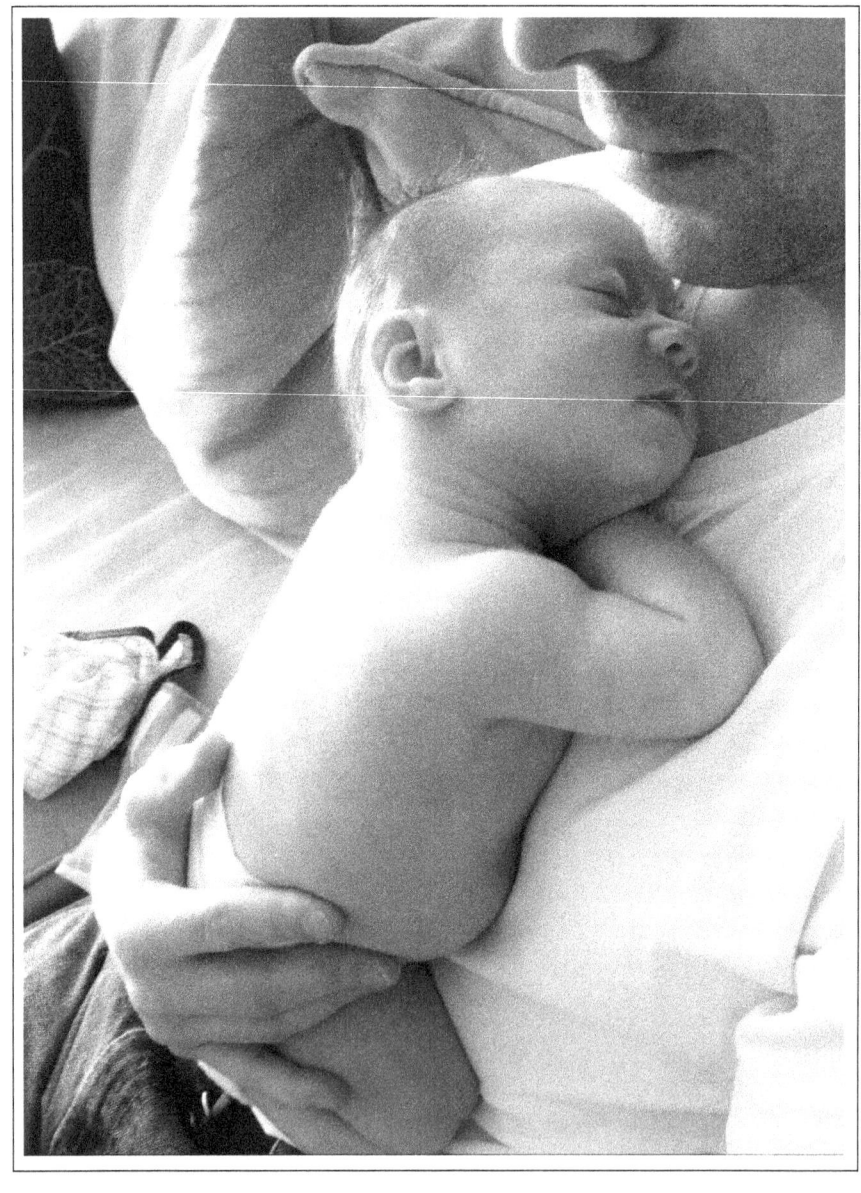

The Book of James
(For Grandson James)

Even before your tiny feet stretched out to welcome
your first moments on this spinning stone,
your destiny lay waiting.

Before you opened your eyes to greet the promise
of a new day, we stood amazed at the mark
you would make upon our hearts.

While you are busy making a place for yourself
in our lives, we have grown to wonder how
we could have ever lived without you.

Though you are on loan to us from the One who
sent you here, we know that your story must
be written, and His will be done.

For now, you are here with us, and just as the
countless waves, an eternal procession, once arrived,
will forever change the waiting shore,
you will forever change who we are.

But as you start on your singular journey ahead,
before you have romanced the wind and shaped
the clouds for your bed, remember our love there will
always be, to guide you through tempestuous days
and to celebrate your every victory.

A Brotherhood Beneath the Elms

Summer afternoons, under the sprawling elms and chestnut trees of New Haven, I learned that the things in life that bind us together are far greater than those things that drive us apart.

Coming from a small city that was also home to one of the world's oldest and most prestigious universities meant, among other things, having the opportunity to experience many cultures and subtle differences in my approach to life.

Growing up on State Street in New Haven afforded me many opportunities. Aside from its easy access to culinary bliss in the occasional slice of a Modern Apizza, I was able to walk the downtown streets of New Haven easily and around the Yale campus, where I could take in the cultural as well as horticultural bonanza that awaited me there.

Every turn up the breezy avenues and down the tree-lined streets bombarded my senses with all kinds of attire, strange languages, music, melding aromas from a variety of eateries, incessant honks, beeps from all manner of transportation, spreads of ivy, and elm trees standing guard over the gated stone walls. The crackling of the leaves under my feet from those same elm trees still echoes in my head, as do the horns and drums of Yale Bowl—welcomed spirits from the simpler days of the past.

I was young, innocent, and unaware that those same ivy-covered walls, outside of which I played and passed the time away dreaming the dreams of innocent youth, protected a world that would prove to be nearly as inaccessible to me as the moon. Wealth, social status, connections, or perhaps just plain good luck—we lacked enough of these things to gain access to the privileged lives of those who conducted their scholarly activities behind the covered walls. It was a time of learning one of the tougher lessons in growing up—opportunity is not equally distributed in life.

From the very first time that I was old enough to walk the four short blocks to the small park where the black kids played ball and hung out, I began sharpening my social skills and learning that underneath their chocolate exteriors beat a heart like mine, which allowed me to run and play under the chestnut trees on those hot summer afternoons, far from the ivy-covered walls on the other side of town. I would learn much later in life that those same walls were equally inaccessible to all of us who sought the comfort of the shady recesses of the park on the hottest of summer afternoons.

Whether old enough to make the trip unassisted or young enough to be chaperoned by an older sibling or occasional parent, we all anticipated meeting up with our monochromatic brethren to play in the wading pool, show off our best baseball cards, and scour the shadowy regions beneath the trees, looking to add to our cache of shiny horse chestnuts. When enough of these treasures had been accumulated, we would punch holes through the biggest and best of the lot, stringing them together with twine to make a collection of horse-chestnut bolas. Once completed, we chose sides and engaged in horse-chestnut bola war, a fight to the death…or at least till dinnertime.

We ran in and out of the shadows, around the perimeter of the park, and occasionally into side streets, throwing our bolas, hoping to catch the legs of our foes and claim victory at least for that afternoon. In truth, our bolas were far less efficient as devices to snare the opponent, but functioned much better as something that could be twirled above our heads to make a weird whooshing sound. It didn't matter; we all felt the excitement of the activity and a certain camaraderie in gathering the chestnuts and creating our weapons for the upcoming battle.

By the end of our afternoon activities, we were all equally tired, dirty, and stained from the green, sticky residue that came from the chestnut husks we had peeled to gather the brown, shiny nuts within. Black, white, green—that was the palette of colors we mixed on those warm summer afternoons as we learned the lessons of horse-chestnut brotherhood.

As the shadows turned deeper and our legs began to grow heavy, we put down whatever remained of our weapons and started the short walk home—black and brown kids in one direction, the rest of us in another. No matter which direction we took, we all walked home to our families, to the smells of supper cooking and the sounds of our moms telling us to clean up for dinner. We did not speak of the conflict we had just endured, nor did we give any hint of our adversaries. We washed our hands and faces, brushed the dust off us, and hoped that our clothes were not too stained to pass a glancing parental inspection before settling down to eat.

After dinner, we escaped the company at the dinner table and slipped away to our bedrooms, got into our pajamas, brushed our teeth, and hopped into bed. Lying there, staring at the ceiling, listening to the hum of the traffic outside our windows on the streets below, and breathing in the intoxicating aroma of pizza cooking in the coal-fired ovens just down the street, we replayed in our heads the adventure from earlier that day as we began to succumb to the evening, anticipating doing battle again the next day.

As our eyes began to close, we thought about the bolas, the horse chestnuts, the pounding of our hearts as we raced around the park that day. We reflected on what we might do differently next time and about our adversaries—their faces, smiles, and laughter. We wondered if they got in trouble for coming home dirty, and we smiled knowing that, whatever the outcome on the battlefield that day, we would be back to do battle again soon if it did not rain... and if our moms let us go.

Since those sultry summer days of my youth, I have seen and experienced many wonderful things in my life, a life in which hope, despair, failure, and victory have been generously apportioned. While the ivy-covered walls still seem as inaccessible to me today as they did in my youth, I still get a rush of excitement each fall when I walk down Elm Street and around New Haven Green.

While many things about New Haven—and me—have changed over the last several decades, the familiarity of the buzzing excitement of New Haven in the fall and the crackling of the leaves under my aging feet provide a reassuring reminder that no matter what fortunes in life we may have amassed, or where life may have taken us, or how much luck and opportunity each of us may have experienced on our journey, home is still found where each of our hearts beats the quickest and where the smell of a New Haven pizza remains as inviting as ever!

Happy Hour at Njoki's

It's been said that God made the earth round so that we cannot see too far down the road. Although there may be skeptics and cynics ready to take issue with the wisdom of the One who left us here, I am thankful that we are only allotted small slices of life at any one time.

It seems that no matter how hard we try, no matter how high we climb, we can only get a glimpse of the next few miles of our life journey. We wonder and wander along a path without knowing for certain where it will lead. For some of us, faith holds that our Creator has minted a plan of good for each of us. While we may not see the purpose or direction for the twists and turns along the way, as believers, we hold fast to the promise of understanding the meaning of our journey when we finally reach our destination.

It was a blistering afternoon as the tour bus made its way into the business district for a half-day of sightseeing, shopping, and cultural enlightenment in the Big Apple of Eastern Africa, Nairobi, Kenya. Taking its name from the Swahili word meaning "place in the sun," Nairobi sits on the banks of the river bearing its name. It is the most notable stop as the river winds its way from the mountains and down through the savanna land, home to the Maasai, the warrior tribe of Eastern Africa.

I had wanted to visit Kenya for quite some time, perhaps even go on safari. Still, I had never gotten the chance until a fortunate convergence of business travel in the Middle East and my desire to kick back for a few days and experience something new and quite different, making this the perfect opportunity to take in some of the unique sights, sounds, and people in this beautiful country. So there I was…finally.

The tour bus unloaded, and I stepped into the dry heat of midday, feeling the shock as I transitioned from my air-conditioned surroundings to the blinding sun. I flipped down the sunglasses and flopped my hat securely onto my head and then began making my way through the maze of people, carts, taxis, and every other conceivable form of human- or animal-powered transportation.

My previous experience with the dark continent had been limited to Morocco, so Nairobi was a new experience, and I was pretty comfortable traveling in unfamiliar places, at least during the daytime and in crowds of people. While in my younger days I might have walked around these places with more bravado, I was always cautious and keenly aware of my surroundings. A little bit of exploration on the banks of the Nairobi seemed in order, so I headed down the street towards the bazaar a few blocks up from the high-rise hotels sitting across from the park.

As I drew closer to the shaded benches where the park began, I could hear the children laughing, car horns honking, and shop owners yelling instructions to the delivery people who had their trucks parked in a long procession, much like airplanes lined up for takeoff. For all its distant intrigue and breathtakingly beautiful pastures, mountains, and colorful people, this could have been a scene from any number of streets in Queens or the Bronx, but this was Nairobi, home to forty-two tribes and where the Kenyan shilling was king.

I made my way through the park as the children ran about chasing each other with swords fashioned from dried tree branches and throwing some odd combination of twine and a type of nut or similar vegetation. It reminded me of my early days back in New Haven, where my friends and I would make bolas out of horse chestnuts and use them to snare our pretend enemies. Reminding me also of those days gone by was the thick smell of diesel fuel and exhaust hanging in the air on sweltering summer days. It was all a little familiar and comforting. All that was missing was the smell of a thin-crust pizza baking in a coal-fired oven and a flickering neon sign reading Budweiser.

I crossed over from the park area and headed past the hotel, where the road began to slope down towards the banks of the river. It was unbearably hot outside now, and I could feel the sun's strength pushing into my head right through my hat, which was already soaked above the brim as my body worked overtime to shed the heat. I needed to find someplace to get out of the sun for a while and take in some cooling rehydration.

As luck would have it, just a half a block or so down the hill from me, I spotted a neon sign with the name Njoki's flashing on and off just above some very familiar neon signage steadily displaying the word Open. So I made my way down the hill with hopes that this was the oasis I needed to step out of the sun and refresh myself.

I turned off the dusty walkway and into the small alcove beneath the flashing sign and grabbed for the large black-metal ring attached to a heavy wooden door secured by equally large black-metal hinges. I pulled on the door to open it, feeling the weight of the door up my entire arm. I braced myself and pulled a bit harder, and the door swung wide open, slamming against the adjacent stone wall in the alcove with a loud thud.

As I inched my way through the portal, the heavy door returned to its closed position with an equally loud thud, leaving me struggling to adjust my vision in the darkness created by the contrast between the bright sunlight from which I had entered and the windowless interior of the bar. My eyes hadn't yet adjusted to my darkened surroundings, but I could hear music in the background, along with the laughter of a woman and a man's voice getting louder, as if to warn me of their approach.

"Welcome to Njoki's, sir," a deep, loud voice proclaimed. "This is the Happy Hour, and for every drink you buy, I give you one for free. What is your pleasure today, sir?" The voice ended in a crescendo that begged for my response.

My eyes had adjusted enough by now to begin taking in my surroundings more fully. I could see the bar more clearly—bottles lined up on display, taps for draft beers at one end, and a Keno game at the other end. There were a handful of people standing at the bar, including a tall, dark, finely dressed man who had draped himself over the shoulder of a woman who continued to laugh intermittently in a voice much louder than the background conversation.

As I continued to adjust to the surroundings, my eyes kept glancing over to the woman seated at the bar and this interesting character beside her who looked as if he had just stepped out of some collector's edition of Nairobi GQ. He was a spectacle in his blue three-piece, pin-striped suit, white-leather shoes, and matching straw hat atop his head. Even in the dimly lit interior, you could easily see his broad white smile and a mouthful of perfectly proportioned teeth accentuated by his contrasting black skin tone. In his hand was a cigarette that he gently held with his thumb and index finger, taking a relaxed, long puff every few minutes, drawing in the toxic smoke with a deliberate and defiant look on his face.

I was still in the middle of my examination when the same voice, now standing behind the bar, asked again, "What can I get for you, sir? Perhaps you are a Scotch drinker? It's Happy Hour at Njoki's all day on Sunday, so you buy one drink, and I'll buy one for you too. What are you going to have, sir?"

I replied, "Whatever light beer you have will be fine," assuming that my answer would satisfy the voice and leave me to consider further what was happening at the end of the bar where I had been focusing my attention.

He continued, "You want English beer, sir, or maybe you'll try something from here in Nairobi, something different. Perhaps some Muratina, you can be a Kikuyu warrior for the day."

He laughed as he turned and walked away, leaving me with no clue what the man with the deep voice would end up pouring for me. Still, at least it ended the exchange; now, I could get back to watching things unfold at the end of the bar.

I collected my beer, took a few swallows, and exhaled a sigh of delight. My parched throat welcomed the frosty flow over my tongue as I slid myself into a chair at the bar, just a couple of seats away from the entertainment I had been following.

About that same time, a young black man came into the bar while I was ordering my drink and took a seat next to me, shouting out to the bartender, "Hey, Eddie, vodka, lime, and soda. Make it quick." Without missing a beat, the young man turned to me, looked past me towards the end of the bar and the impeccably dressed man and laughing woman I had been watching. The young man threw back his head, closed his eyes, and let out a laugh that seemed to explode from his body. He gathered himself as his drink was delivered, dropping his head into his hands and then raising it again to look around, quietly sipping his drink in the process.

I was beginning to wonder just what kind of place it was that I had chosen to refresh myself. Njoki's seemed friendly enough, but something was going on here involving the finely dressed, broadly smiling black man in the suit and hat.

Just as I started contemplating the possibilities, the young man sitting next to me put his hand on my left shoulder and leaned into me. "I guess Smoke'n Jimmy got himself another lady to love," he said quietly to me.

"Oh, you mean the tall man at the end of the bar in the suit?" I asked politely.

"Yes, he is quite the man. He is in here every Sunday about this time; I don't think I have ever seen that man with the same lady more than once." The young man continued, "He comes here from church every Sunday after he takes the collection. He doesn't even wait for the church service to finish, and he is on his way here to Njoki's for the rest of the afternoon."

While I was listening to the young man, I began to look around and study the place more closely. There were trophies of one kind or another placed on shelves behind the bar area. In between were framed pictures, some of people laughing in a group, some on the river in a boat with a sign hanging off the ship reading Celebrate Nairobi—Sponsored by Njoki's Bar and Pub. On the wall next to that picture was a sign that read The NFL Plays Here. I began thinking to myself how popular the National Football League had become, reaching to the Dark Continent, until I could make out the smaller letters on the sign—Nairobi Football League followed by the image of a soccer ball.

My wandering gaze was again interrupted by the young man to my left as he put his hand on my shoulder once more. "You know the story of Smoke'n Jimmy?" he asked me. Before I could respond, he just continued, "He used to be some kind of official in the government here, something to do with business and shops and the Kenyan government." He took another sip of his drink, smiled, and continued, "But he got thrown out a few years ago; he got caught taking money from people who paid him to help them get a business license."

Whatever beer it was that I had been served, it was doing the trick, and I began to feel cooler and more relaxed as I sat quietly at the bar, listening to the young man next to me.

He continued, "Yeah, Smoke'n Jimmy was a big shot. He comes in here two or three times a week with a different woman on his arm. He would talk all loud and buy drinks for the ladies and get those girls smiling and laughing like they all were school kids." He looked down into his drink and finished, "No, he don't brag so much no more."

We sat in silence for a minute. I took the opportunity to finish my beer and motioned to the deep-voiced bartender that I wanted to settle my tab as I prepared to leave the bar.

In one motion, the bartender ripped the receipt off the machine, reached forward with my check in hand, and asked me in the same deep, loud voice, "You ain't taking your free drink, sir?" He reminded me again, "Sunday is Happy Hour all day at Njoki's. You by one drink, and I buy you the next."

I politely answered, "No, I'm fine with just this one," making sure to respond in a firm but appreciative voice as the bartender turned back away from me, leaving a hint of disappointment on his face.

I gathered my belongings from on top of the bar, drained the last few swallows from my beer bottle, and turned to my left to slide out of my chair. Settling onto my feet, I flopped my hat back onto my head, picked up my sunglasses off the bar, and adjusted my clothes as I readied to head back out into the afternoon sun and the melting heat. As I turned to walk towards the door, I couldn't resist the opportunity to turn back around to the young man who had been sitting next to me. I returned the favor by putting my right hand on his shoulder, leaning into him, and quietly asking him a question: "So why is he named Smoke'n Jimmy?" The young man didn't respond immediately, so I offered up another question: "Is it because he stands at the bar holding a cigarette in that very peculiar way?"

The young man burst into laughter once again, shaking his head from side to side, dropping his head back into his hands in a sign of resignation, or maybe he didn't know how to satisfy my curiosity. He quieted himself once again, pulling his head out of the palms of his hands, lifting his glass to his mouth for another sip. Pausing a moment, he turned to me and looked deep into my eyes. A hint of a smile began to appear on his face as he quietly spoke.

"Jimmy, over there, he has been coming in here for a long time. He's been romancing the ladies, doing deals and favors, and telling everybody what they want to hear; he's been to lots of places we have no clue about. When he's got a few extra dollars, he buys a round of drinks for the bar, and everybody yells, 'Hey, Jimmy, you're smokin', man!' Then Jimmy flashes that big white smile, and that black face lights up like a Christmas tree."

Not wanting to settle for less than a full explanation for Jimmy's unusual nickname, I pressed the young man one more time. "But why the name, why Smoke'n Jimmy?" I asked again.

My drinking companion's face softened, his voice deepened, and his gaze fell to the floor as he continued, "Man, nobody that comes in this place ever been much more than fifty miles from their home, except if they been in the army or moved away for some job in a different place. They have all been born on some farm in the country or lived in town all their lives. Those who have money and send their kids to school in other places don't come into Njoki's. Nope, just us folk here. Our world is as far as Smoke'n Jimmy's smile and that glowing cigarette in his fingers." Then he continued, "To tell you the truth, most people here got no damn clue if half of what Smoke'n Jimmy says he done is true or not. They don't care."

"Why do you say that?" I asked.

My young friend followed that with "The way I see it, we all got a little bit of Smoke'n Jimmy in us. We've all done things that we've been proud of, and we've done some things that we find out later ain't such a good idea. We come into Njoki's; we order a drink; we have a few laughs; we tell some stories; maybe we find a little romance sometimes. Nobody sitting on these barstools is judging anybody else. We're all just listening and watching. When we leave here, we all feel like our world got a little bigger, just for a while." He continued, "Tell you the truth, I ain't got no damn idea how Smoke'n Jimmy got that name. I know that when I see him, he's gonna make me laugh, and when I leave here, I will be smiling too." He finished with "You understand that, friend?"

I made the final turn towards the door, giving a parting gesture to my drinking companion, who had already turned back to the bar to order another drink. As I opened the heavy door to the outside world, I could feel the heat of the day again. I reluctantly stepped slowly through the entry alcove and onto the street, heading down towards where the bus had been parked.

As I began to walk back to the bus, I swear that I could hear in the distance voices shouting, "Hey Jimmy, you're smoke'n." It made me smile, and I remembered that we are all like the waves we see coming ashore. We are all made of the same basic form and substance. While our journey is a singular one, we do not travel alone, and like the waves, as the waiting shore greets them, we change everything that we touch in our lives, and we too are changed by the journey. Keep on smoke'n, Jimmy!

Time and Tide

In this endless procession of time, we come to know more about ourselves and how we fit into the mosaic of living. We realize that each of us, though unique and singular in form, is a finely cut jewel set into a predetermined and exacting position in the crown of creation.

Rather than ponder whether our life experiences have been predetermined or if all of what happens to us is nothing more than a series of random occurrences, let us instead consider the possibility that, however it is that we get from one point in life to another, our existence was not by chance but by design.

The experiences that befall us in our daily lives are like drops of water; each can reflect an image of the world around us.

But it is only through the sum of these droplets, like the ocean, that we see a bigger picture of life and gain insights into ourselves and where we are positioned in the vastness of creation.

As time passes, we continue to accumulate experiences. We gain more insight and clarity into our living and the reason for our existence.

We come to understand that the path we have traveled, the experiences we have gathered, and even the insights we have gained are all just one tick away from the past, and that what matters most is not how we have spent the time in the past, but what we do now, moving forward with whatever time remains in our journey before it is all used up.

Dreamer's Soliloquy

If I had to choose how to live each new day, I would choose to see sunshine every step of the way. I would watch the sun's arrival into grey morning skies. I would listen more closely to birds on the fly.

I would think of my children and their lives now afar, of things that they said when they wished on a star. I would ponder the eyes of my grandsons, so bright, with their visions and dreams as they entered the night.

I would sing a new song every day of the week. I would summon my smiles, each hour, to repeat. I would conjure up love, simple, timeless, and true. I would give in to passion and the things lovers do.

I would end the day softly in the arms of my love and whisper thanksgiving to the One up above. I would fall asleep grateful for having the time to ask you again, dear life, "Dance with me, into the sublime!"

New Awakening

In the still desert air, beneath an ancient etched peak, a flower awakens from her solitary sleep.

Her eyes lifting upward, growing wide in the virgin light, she has beaten the shadows, the specters of night.

Claiming now weathered peaks, endless skies for her home, she celebrates life singularly, but never alone.

Embracing the new day, she puts to rest, at long last, the remnants, the memories, the salty rains of the past.

With confidence and purpose, she strains for the light, her spirit now ready for the uncertain flight.

To seek out her fate somewhere between earth and sky, she travels with song and a peaceful heart. Companions forever, they fly!

Glowing Embers

As the heat of summer begins to wane and the days shorten, the changing of seasons can be heard in the song of the crickets as they bid farewell to the sultry nights of summer and plan their welcoming chorus for the cooler nights of autumn nearly upon us.

It's a time of the year when we can more fully experience with our senses the forward movement of this rock upon which we stand as it makes its way on a prescribed course through the blackness of space. The air around us begins to chill, and the trees take on a new palette of colors before shedding their delicate collection of leaves to the hardening ground that beckons below.

Our silent walks of summer sunrises are now replaced with the crackling of leaves and the whooshing of the autumn winds through the tree branches above as they hasten to reveal their near-naked forms like unashamed and exuberant lovers.

For those of us whose number of trips around our parent star have sufficient weight, memories of Kate Hepburn and Golden Pond come to mind and enliven within us the visions of peaceful sunsets, the calling of the loons, and the warmth of a fire burning within our hearts—an inextinguishable love and a symbol of an unspoken but enduring partnership.

As the number of our trips around our parent star increases and our outward vision becomes dim, we develop a much keener ability to see within. We feel the intensity of the seasons more deeply as we recall the memories and the secret callings of our hearts.

In the glow of embers that relegates the evening shadows into faint images, our minds run through all that has gone before us—our victories, and our disappointments. The promises we made to ourselves and to others are all examined in the dimming light, each assigned to a particular tick of the clock and a specific step of our journey.

We begin to understand the order of importance of things in our lives. We see each new day as a beautifully wrapped gift to be opened and shared with those around us. We hear the laughter of our children and grandchildren, and we fixate on the sparkle in their eyes as they prepare for the surprise and wonder that is life. We stand guard over them and pledge our love and protection without compromise or delay.

Taking advantage of the time to reflect, we examine who we are, what we have done and accomplished, what we have left undone, and what dreams we still hold deep within the quiet recesses of our hearts. In the silence of this season, amid the dying embers and recollections of those moments in life that have left the deepest marks upon our souls, we come to a new realization.

We begin to understand that our appreciation for Kate Hepburn, a golden pond, and the change of season is but a manifestation of our desire to find a belonging, to have the reassurance that we are not alone. We understand, too, that what matters most in life is not in which cycle of our years it is that we find this assurance, but that we recognize and embrace it whenever it comes into our lives.

Hopefully, we have learned from the passing seasons and the many steps of our journey that we must cherish each moment of existence, each fallen leaf, and every step of our journey forward with a peaceful heart and a willingness to share our blessings with those who along with us share each sunrise, each sunset, and each tick of the clock.

Starry Night

Vincent Van Gogh offered us an alternative in viewing the heavens under which we draw our day to a close each evening. My amazement is unending each time that I gaze up at a clear night sky and allow myself to take in the fullness of the heavens sparkling above me.

It is a palette awash with twinkling specks across the blackness, with wisps of milky starlight whipped into a broad stroke that stretches our imagination as much as it does our visual acuity.

My head is filled with numbers: two trillion galaxies, two hundred billion stars in each, and countless planets whirling through space. The sheer number of objects in the universe is well beyond our collective abilities to comprehend. So we draw in a deep breath, shake our heads in wonder, and ponder the big questions of our existence.

We are fearful, in part, that we are not alone in this universe. The reality may be that we are not as special and unique a specimen of creation as we perhaps once thought.

The inverse is equally unsettling. In the mind-numbing vastness of creation, all we may have to illuminate the blackness surrounding the twisting blue stone we share is each other and the starlight that falls upon us.

Perhaps, then, it would be more beneficial for us to turn our attention away from the shadowy expanse above our heads, focusing instead on the threads of reality and oneness of creation into which we have been carefully woven.

In so doing, maybe we will discover and learn to appreciate that we are individual grains of sand on the beach of humankind, drawing strength and courage from our common beginnings, and wonder and expectation from our shared destiny, and that what lies in the depths of space isn't nearly as important as what lies within our hearts.

Still Waters

Amid the ever-present uncertainties and chaos of our present-day lives, it's little wonder that we may long for a return to a simpler time—a time free from the issues, decisions, and responsibilities of each day.

We strain to understand the disruption of the present moment that runs through us like an unwelcome and inescapable surge—a flood of bad news, worry, and unsettledness that seeps its way into the darkened recesses of our minds and fills our hearts with a watery emptiness.

We turn to each other for answers, but we find only the mirrored expressions of our confusion and anxiety. We then turn away in resentment, disappointed that others have been unable to explain what we have been incapable of understanding.

In times such as these, when we are amid the storm, we often fail to realize that the waves tossing us about at the height of peril are of similar form and substance as those upon which we glided to safe harbor, testing not the waves but how we navigated our way through them.

While the waters may be rough and our boat may roll and heave precariously, the waters of confusion and uncertainty are not unknown to any of us. Different storms and different times have proven the depth of our spirit.

Despite the waters upon which we ride in these turbulent days, we know that there is a calm, a peace that exists below what we can see on the surface. The calm and the peace we long for are anchored in our faith, in the reassurance that our Creator has promised us salvation, not only from the world around us, but also from the world within us!

Crab on a Leash

The warm sands and relentless trade winds of the Netherlands Antilles always provide me with the opportunity to dream, to learn, and to experience life and its oddities in a way that seems to come more easily in a place far removed from the pace and problems of day-to-day living back on the mainland.

Over the twenty-plus years of visiting this desert gem, shining in its familiar turquoise waters and enduring the unstoppable trade winds, I have grown to learn much about the island and the people who initially inhabited this speck of heaven. Aruba, a small island nestled in the southern Caribbean Sea just north of Venezuela, boasts a history as vivid as its turquoise waters. Long before European ships dotted the horizon, Aruba was home to the Caquetío, an Arawak-speaking, Indigenous people who arrived from mainland South America. They sustained themselves through fishing, hunting, and simple agriculture, living in harmony with the arid but sun-drenched land, and left behind remarkable petroglyphs in the island's caves.

Spanish explorers first landed on Aruba in 1499, claiming it for the Spanish crown. However, finding little gold, they dubbed it an "island of giants" due to the tall stature of its native inhabitants. For over a century, Aruba remained under Spanish rule, serving as a refuge for pirates and a waypoint for explorers. The Dutch seized Aruba in 1636 and established a colonial presence that endures to this day. Over the centuries, Aruba's population became a unique blend of Indigenous, European, and African heritage, shaped by waves of migration and trade. Today, the island's vibrant culture and welcoming spirit reflect this rich and varied past, making Aruba a true crossroads of Caribbean history.

Before I proceed, it's essential for me to remind you that island life differs significantly from our daily lives and routines in numerous ways. There are differences here in the islands that are far less subtle than one would experience back home when contrasting life in the country with that in a city. The entire context, the frame of reference for island living, is so vastly different from what we usually experience that we sometimes struggle to make sense of what we see around us.

What draws us, then, to these exotic retreats? The sun is great, but unless you are very careful, you will suffer the burning consequences. The long stretches of white beach and warm turquoise waters are beautiful and inviting, but the sand can be hot on the feet, and the salt is unkind to one's eyes. The trade winds are cooling, but they persist and buffet one with an exfoliating skin treatment rivaling that of a chic spa. So what is it then that draws us here?

It's the people watching that beckons us, the endless parade of the tanned, the topless, and the occasional clueless. It's the interaction between tourists and locals, lifestyles colliding like some momentous event in cultural tectonics. This is where things get interesting.

Years of visiting the island have reshaped my outlook on life and daily routine. A series of career changes and failed relationships left me restless, so when I had the chance to buy a small getaway and make it my home for a week each year, I seized it.

My life used to be a wild jumble of job swaps and cringeworthy dates—I was auditioning for Most Likely to Get Lost in a Midlife Crisis…again! But the island? It's my yearly rescue mission. Suddenly, coffee tastes fresher, mornings are less offensive, and my biggest worry is whether seagulls will stage another heist on my lunch.

Each visit, I'm reminded that sunburns fade, but questionable life choices make for excellent stories around a beach bonfire. The island hasn't just brightened my mood; it's given me enough comic mishaps to fill a sitcom. I no longer see in my dreams a headstone marking my demise with the chiseled proclamation, "Here Lies Joe Korzon, of Noble Heart and Unceasing Desire to Alienate Every Woman in the World, One Divorce at a Time."

So it was that morning in Aruba, as I headed out for my ritual 9:00 a.m. walk along the beach, following the same plan as earlier in the week and the day before, and so on. Life in the islands is at the very least predictable, perhaps resulting from the consistent weather and eternal holiday atmosphere. So what could be so different on this day? Would the sun be any less bright? Would the skirting waves be any less seductive? Would the firm, tanned breasts of the young Venezuelan women be any less inviting? I think not. So what is it, then, that would make that ritual walk along the beach that day quite different?

During my morning stroll along the beach—trying not to trip over a small fleet of idle WaveRunners—I noticed a young local man perched serenely near the water's edge. He was so focused on whatever he was doing that I half expected him to be summoning a genie from a bottle. As I drew closer, the mystery unfolded: he was wielding one end of a surprisingly long piece of twine, the other tied securely around a fiddler crab roughly four inches in size. It turned out this crab was his companion for the morning; they were embarking on an adventure through rocks and shallow surf, the crab at the end of a makeshift leash.

Not wanting to seem nosy—or, worse, a disapproving tourist—I opened with an innocuous, "Beautifully quiet this morning, isn't it?"

He grinned, his eyes never leaving the crustacean. "Yes, very quiet today," he replied. Then, as if reading my baffled expression, he added, "Most folks are in town, attending a funeral for one of the guys here. He got killed the other day on his motorcycle. I'm just watching his things." He gave the crab's leash a gentle tug for emphasis.

I couldn't resist. "So…is crab walking a local sport? Or is he training for some crustacean Olympics?"

The young man chuckled, shaking his head. "He's got no ambitions—just likes exploring. Better than riding jet skis,

I think. Better than racing motorcycles, for sure. I used to fix these machines for the guy who got killed. Don't know what I'm gonna do now. So I play with this bit of crab, and it keeps my mind off the ugly stuff."

There was something quietly profound about that: two companions—one human, one crab—finding solace in the rhythm of tide and sand while life's commotions unfolded elsewhere. He didn't try to sell me a Jet Ski ride or push any tourist trinkets. Instead, his entire focus rested on guiding this little crab in and out of the surf, utterly content in their simple pastime.

As I walked away, I found myself reflecting on how familiar it felt—the desire to slow down and attend to small joys, even when the larger world buzzes with deadlines, grief, and obligations. Sometimes, the best way to keep watch over life's valuables is to hold a crab by a string and let the morning unfold. Maybe things here aren't quite as different from home as I thought!

A Celebration of Light

We only begin living once we realize that each of us is beautifully and wonderfully made, that we need neither the approval nor even the recognition of others to shine as bright as any star in the heavens.

Our Creator, in His love and divine plan of good for us, has breathed into each of us all that we need to nurture the seeds of greatness growing within us. To deny those seeds is to deny the light of the universe, which has been set aside for each of us, a light that each one of us reflects into our universe in thanksgiving and in praise to the One who left us here.

It is a light to illuminate our path through the darkest moments of our lives and to chase away the clouds that would deny us our victory. It is the reflected light of faith in our Creator and of our love for one another.

Let us rejoice, then, and fully embrace the unique aspects of our individuality. Let us join hands in brotherhood and thanksgiving, committed to a new reality in which every eye is clear to the wonders of the night sky, every ear is attuned to the song of life in the wind, and every heart is open to the beauty and diversity of creation and of all who are a part of it!

Peaceful Hearts

In her book *The Joy in Loving: A Guide to Daily Living*, Mother Teresa offered us a path to finding a peaceful heart through diligently living a life of respect for all life and all people. She loved unconditionally, and she lived in humility.

She rarely spoke about herself, focusing instead on the needs of others and on the hard work she had chosen for herself in living out her mission in life with great dignity and attuned to the dignity of others, no matter how forgotten or disliked they might be.

We live in a world where boundaries for decency, respect, tolerance, and civility are vanishing; an "everyone for themselves" mentality prevails. If we are to become all that our Creator has planned for us to be as individuals and as a species, then we must start healing from within and looking at the world around us through the eyes of those with whom we share this twisting stone upon which we ride through space.

That, to me, is the essence of finding passion in life's wrinkles as we navigate the wormholes of our universe in search of a deeper meaning to our existence. It is an attempt to connect the pieces of our daily living into a strand of shiny memories, like pearls, that will adorn our lives and endure the scrutiny of our reflection and self-assessment. Each new dawn brings with it an opportunity to discover yet another tiny globe to sew on our string.

Every morning, we breach the silence of the new day by giving thanks and praise to our Creator; then we become slaves to the daily routines that find their way into our lives with both subtle and profound impact. If we are not careful, over time our routines become an integral part of our lives and, in many ways, help define us, or at the very least, paint a picture of how we wish to be perceived by others.

Though life may provide us with an opportunity to jump from cloud to cloud as we move forward on our journey, it remains our responsibility to gather up all the lessons and experiences of our travels and to squeeze out a few drops of insight that can somehow improve our lives as well as the lives of those whom we meet along the way.

While our Creator's plan for each of us may include unequal portions of opportunity and challenge, it is by our own hands and determination, by our faith, and by living in humility and thanksgiving that we magnify our blessings in whatever form and quantity they may be. In so doing, we fulfill our purpose in living: to love one another without judgment or precondition.

Though we may not be known to one another, we are nonetheless connected by the threads of humanity and by divine design. We may rise and move to the ebb and flow of our individual fortunes, but we are at our best when we choose to endure, to sustain, and to celebrate together as one.

Benevolent Messenger

To My Guardian Angel

As we ride this twisting stone through space and time, I become more aware of your benevolence and of your gentle hand leading me towards the light of a new day.

With each passing sun and welcoming moon, I feel the breath of your assurance on my neck, like whispers riding the breeze through fields of wheat, silently cutting delicate rivulets into the golden shafts, pointing the way forward, pointing the way home.

I raise my eyes to the heavens, and I feel the welcoming warmth, another sunrise to fill my soul with the promise of this new dawn and to celebrate the joy awaiting me in your watchful care and unceasing love.

Fate has determined that we share this speck of stone and embark together on a common journey, so we move into tomorrow, one step, one day at a time towards the promise of our shared destiny.

For in His love, our Creator has given you to me, and in His wisdom, He has provided that the mountains in life, which are too high for me to climb alone, we shall ascend together!

Sweet Discovery

Lily and Rose

It matters not whether the Lily exalts the Rose or if the Rose graces the Lily; if both are strong, they will stand tall together in the garden through tempest and time.

In the confidence of their commitment and love, they will share the wonder of countless dawns, taking nourishment from one another and finding shade and comfort in each other's company.

They will feast on moonlight and gentle breezes, toasting to their dreams under a blanket of twinkling specks of heaven, dancing in the evening shadows with playful exuberance.

There, they will watch the moon climb its way across a sky spotted with silvery wisps, and they will give way to the passions and beauty of their substance.

Gently entwined, they will lie beside one another, vulnerable, covered only by the covenant that binds them, bathed in the sweetness and scent of their creation, confident in the silence and flow of life between them.

They will slumber in the gentle darkness, finding purpose and renewal in the shadows of the night, waiting for the first hints of the new dawn to come softly upon them.

Together, they will live out their destiny on the promise that every day will be a dream of fulfilled happiness and that every tomorrow will be a vision of their unimagined joy.

Outlook on Life

One of the earliest lessons we learn from the moment we claw our way out of the womb is that life isn't fair. While we share a common ultimate destiny, the paths upon which we travel through life are as unique as our fingerprints.

Perhaps we were born into a life of privilege, or maybe one filled with challenges and significant obstacles to overcome; whatever the case, we may feel disadvantaged at times and may even wonder why we were ever pinned to this twisting stone.

Life is a collective and all-inclusive journey. For sure, our progress as individuals is measured by our steps, but our progress as a species is a collective effort.

While we don't know the exact number of our days, we can be certain that each day is ordained with a purpose for every minute and for each breath we take. Every breath, every heartbeat, every smile, and each tear that we shed are all counted and help to shape the world we all share and the quality of our daily lives.

No matter where our paths in life may lead us or what the exact number of our days here may be, our covenant with life is to learn, to love, to inspire one another, to humble ourselves, and to bring us all closer to one another and to the One who left us here.

Our Creator is faithful to His word and all His promises. His plan of good for each of us includes happiness, fullness of life, peace, and joy. Our job is to have faith in those promises and to be faithful to our responsibilities, acting with "right" thinking and empathetic behavior.

These things may seem more challenging to embrace on a cold winter morning or with a raging virus on our doorstep, but we need to remind ourselves that rain falls on the just as well as on the unjust. Even in the cold and rainy misery of the present, it is our responsibility to do our part to stay dry, put up an umbrella, wear a raincoat, and look for sunny weather.

Opening our eyes to the beauty of life around us in all its forms and to the commonality of our shared destiny can soften the edges of the world we are experiencing at present.

If we stay true to our faith in our Creator's plan of good for each of us, we can be confident that we will see a bright new day and again feel the warmth of a welcoming sunrise, no matter how much rain has fallen in the dark of night!

Rainy-Day Malaise

I've heard it said that a broken heart sometimes is a good thing, that only when the heart is broken can light find its way in between the cracks to allow the pieces to be reassembled into something grander and more beautiful.

It's safe to say that life will provide each of us ample opportunity at some point or another to experience the pain of disappointment, a love lost, or perhaps a dream unrealized.

It's not easy being Cheerleader for the World; no one tells you what the score is or when the game is over. They marvel at your spirit, your energy, and your genuine love for people, but the rest you are left to figure out on your own.

When we give so much of ourselves to others, it's no wonder that we may feel emptied at times. But that same love and energy for life that we unselfishly share with others in friendship, caring, and acts of kindness has the power to sustain us during those moments of silent reflection and darkness.

While these moments of tribulation are as natural and necessary for our growth and transformation, as are the dreary days and spring rains to the beauty that awaits, it is with the flowers that will follow the days of rain and gloom that we will be renewed, refreshed, and rendered able to once again stand tall in the garden to brighten the world, as is our destiny and our Creator's plan of good for each of us. Shine on!

Olde Wood

Slowly, I wake up to the call of the new day. I feel unprepared though I have practiced this moment in my thoughts with equal parts trepidation and enthusiasm—perhaps a bit less of the latter as the days grow longer—and I struggle to awaken and face fully the reality of the present.

In the past, I have weathered life's storms without compromise. Silently, I have withstood the torrents of tears that pulled at my roots, threatening to fell me and deny me my destiny, my final victory.

I have embraced each sunrise, shrugging off the heat of summer nights as well as the chill of wintry nights. I have witnessed each sunset and slumbered beneath a blanket of twinkling stars—moments of selfishness—yet I was constantly aware of my responsibilities to those who gathered beneath my protective cover.

Do not forsake me though my outside is dry and riddled with cracks and imperfections that grow more obvious each day, though my limbs creak and moan from the number and weight of the days laid upon me. I still find joy and passion for providing comfort and a brief refuge from the harshness of life for those whom it has been my mission to guard, to nurture, and to love unconditionally, as intended by the One who planted me here.

Olde Wood

Slowly, I awoke to the call of dawn,
A practiced moment, trepidation drawn.
Enthusiasm wanes as days grow long.
I strain to greet the present, right or wrong.
Storms have weathered me, tears have flowed,
Yet I have stood firm; my roots have grown.
Each sunrise met, each sunset seen,
A moment's peace beneath a starry sheen.
Though dry and cracked, my limbs are worn.
I still find joy, a passion reborn
To offer comfort, refuge, and embrace.
A mission is given in this sacred space.

Where the Sweet Spirits Dwell

Early one summer morning, when the air was still and sweet with the promise of a new day and the approaching dawn, a man journeyed along the water's edge in a cadence of purposeful strides.

As he skirted the intruding waves and detoured around the occasional renegade palm frond, he left behind him, in the firm wet sand, deep and undeniable footprints acknowledging his heavy and troubled heart.

Pressing on up the beach with a look of both determination and uncertainty, he continued his trek, oblivious to his surroundings until his eyes strayed upward, where they found in the distance a singular figure perched quietly above a large outcropping of rocks by the water's edge.

As the man drew closer to the outcropping, in the light of the emerging dawn, he could make out more clearly an angelic vision waiting quietly for the dawn's full arrival. In the growing light, the man could see an ageless winged figure dressed in a long, flowing robe that blended seamlessly with all it touched in soft, radiant white light.

As the man slowly walked closer to satisfy his curiosity, the apparition turned to him and looked deeply into his eyes. With a gentle smile and a soothing voice, it quietly proclaimed, "That which you seek is here, all around you!"

Accepting this sudden proclamation and the mysterious vision before him, the man recoiled but gathered himself enough to respond in a polite and pained voice, "Oh, heavenly vision, guardian angel divine, I have lost someone dear to me, and I have embarked upon this journey to find that secret place where the sweet spirits dwell, for surely my dear one resides there."

The angelic vision turned away from the man and again looked out over the water, pointing to where a wave had gently broken and disappeared into the waiting shore. In a practiced but understanding tone, the vision again proclaimed, "Behold the endless procession of waves. Each is born of similar substance and direction, yet each one finds its own time and place to come ashore. In so doing, each wave leaves its unique mark on the sand, conveying its singular energy and essence upon all it touches."

Upon hearing this, the man once again gathered himself and in a polite though confused voice again replied to the vision, "Divine one, you misunderstood me. As you can see, we share this place only with the rocks, the sand, the sky, and the water. The dear one for whom I search must surely gather in some other location. Perhaps you can point the way?"

Turning once again towards the man, the angelic vision smiled lovingly, stretched wide its arms, white robes flowing in the wind, looked deeply into the man's eyes, and with an eternally patient voice responded, "Sweet child, look around you. Can you not see what is right in front of you—that which you look for? As it is with those things you see here around you, so too it is with your loved one and all of the other sweet spirits who have found their way ashore.

"Like the waves you see in the distance, along their journey, they have endured both tempest and the blackness of night. They have faithfully gathered the light and the promise of each new dawn, and they have dreamed of both happiness and despair. They have struggled onward, through the rhythm of life, finding both solitude in their singular journey and solace in the company of uncountable others who, like the waves you see here, have converged and come ashore. And like the waiting shore, you have been touched, embraced, and forever changed, as the essence that is their spirit has become one with yours. Your lives, your destinies forever entwined."

The vision continued, "Sweet child, that which you seek is close at hand. Your journey should take you no further than the distance between your heart and mind. There, on that road, is where your dear one awaits, and you may visit him at any time. Sweet child, look within and welcome your loved one. There, the two of you shall rejoice in your love for one another, and you shall sing the songs of life, both past and present, in chorus with all the other sweet spirits. Rejoice, my child, your search has ended!"

Upon hearing this, the man felt the radiance of the new day come upon him. Looking down, in the warming sand near his feet, he spied a silver-dollar-sized stone. Picking it up, he paused for a moment and then launched the stone into the rush of the oncoming waves; it skipped once, then again, and disappeared into the frothy water.

As he turned to walk back up the beach, the man glanced over his shoulder to where the vision had been, but he found himself alone with the rocks, the sky, and the sea. Turning again back up the beach, the man now broke into a relaxed smile, noticing that the heavy footprints of his journey had been transformed into soft pools, gently reminding him of his way back home.

Pivot Point

Psychiatrist and author Elisabeth Kübler-Ross wrote, "People are like stained glass windows. They sparkle and shine when the sun is out, but when the darkness sets in, their true beauty is revealed only if there is light from within."

We seem to shine more easily when our path is clear and our direction is fixed in our minds. We become more resolute in our thinking and our actions, feeling energized and acting with purpose.

But when our path is uncertain and we can only see a few feet in front of us, we become anxious, even fearful, at times as we sense a loss of control and vulnerability.

For those who stay open to the lessons of life come to a common understanding that we cannot control what happens around us but only that which is within us.

However, it is while life unfolds for us that we inevitably come to a point where our way forward is obscured and uncertain. We become unsettled and unsure of our next steps as we peer into the darkness around us.

It is at these moments that we must make a choice: to battle for control of the people and the circumstances facing us, or to willingly relinquish control of our situation to a higher power and find the light within ourselves that will illuminate our way forward.

While some may view this choice as choosing to act with courage and determination versus acting out of a sense of weakness and withdrawal, we are reminded that our faith demands the strength and resolution to let go and to let the one who left us here be that light within us that will show us the way forward and soothe our worried minds.

To those who have survived crashing into life's unseen barriers, hold on to your courage and your desire to navigate through the turbulence of life's twisting journey and exquisite wrinkles. Within those wrinkles and the unanticipated twists and turns of your daily living, you can discover the true passions of your heart and your real purpose for living.

Remember also that the journey is neither for the faint of heart nor for those who lack perseverance or purpose of action.

The journey demands our attention to the hazards and to the victories we encounter along the way, as well as our willingness to change direction for the glory of our Creator and the benefit of our fellow travelers.

The Book of Chaos

Life Lesson #1—Chaos Rules!

The spinning rock upon which we all live makes its way effortlessly around our star on a predictable path and has done so for countless billions of years.

Yet science teaches us that our distance from the sun, the tilt of our planet, as well as its rotational speed, are constantly changing. Even our sun will change over time to swell in size and eventually devour our very insignificant planet sometime in the very distant future.

The dilemma for all of us in this learning is that, even as we experience living in measured moments, with expected outcomes and neatly stored memories, almost everything around and within us is constantly changing.

The appearance of order in our universe and our lives is an illusion. We live in a constant state of change. Everything we have learned since taking our first breath in the changing atmosphere continues to be redefined, reshaped, and repositioned for our future use and understanding as we step forward on our journey through life.

Each of us then reacts to the changes around us and within us in a never-ending dance with chaos as we bump into one another like spinning tops on a table. Our predictability within our daily routines also changes; so too does the predictability of those with whom we share our journey.

Finding patterns in chaos allows us to grasp insights into living that have immediate value to us at any point on our journey through life; if we understand that, what we learn today, like us, only has a limited lifespan.

Another Brick in the Wall

Life calls us into action. Every success and failure and each challenge provides us with an opportunity to grow beyond our self-imposed limitations, but only if we can transform our thinking as we move forward on our life journey.

Sensitivity and Passion are two different lenses in the same pair of glasses. Each is used to view life differently, but both focus our eyes on our journey rather than on what we have accumulated along the way.

At a time of year when we tend to glance back over our shoulders in reflection on yet another journey completed around our parent star, it's easy to become critical of ourselves regarding the progress we've made down our chosen paths in life.

While self-examination and measuring progress against our immediate and longer-term plans for our lives are helpful, we need to remind ourselves to broaden our vision of progress to include not just what we can count around us, but the value of what we have discovered within us.

We don't all need to walk the Great Wall of China to find passion in our lives; it's often within an arm's reach if we just open our eyes and our minds to those simple wrinkles in the fabric of our everyday lives.

A great cup of coffee and a sunrise, a cocktail shared in the beauty of companionship, our feet firmly planted in the warm beach sand, a special meal, a golden sunset, the hugs and laughter of our children and our grandchildren—if we can't find passion in these things, then we surely won't find it in some exotic destination.

In a year that has been dominated by issues of virus, violence, disappointment, and despair, let us not overlook our victories and our invincibility as we came together to respond to life's challenges, to drive out the illness within our bodies and our minds.

As we open ourselves to the possibilities of what we can be and what we can experience in the new year, let us also remember that our most significant victories in life are often found on the road between heart and mind, and they come from our willingness to touch the hearts of others, helping them find comfort and meaning in their days and each step of their journey.

Inside each of us, our Creator has planted seeds of greatness. It is our mission in life to nurture and grow those seeds to maturity for our benefit and the benefit of others. While not all of us share the same seeds, at harvest we all reap the good that sustains each of us and all of our brothers and sisters!

Silent Passage

In the quiet of the evening, my mind drifts back to a time when my days were filled with experiences stretching out over many continents and countless hours of silent escape from one cloud top to the next.

There was a time when I sat over outstretched silvery wings that welcomed the first few strands of dawn as they climbed into the frigid sky above the grey Norwegian Sea. It was a moment of both stark contrast and reflection.

Once again, remembering the high above the ash and glowing lava that is the geology of Iceland, I rush towards Greenland, a place where name and landscape conspire in a cruel flip-flop of reality. I am heading home from my India experience; though unshaven and a bit ragged, I am at peace.

My time with friends, both known and yet to be met, has been short, but I have stayed long enough to find reassurance in my perceptions about this enchanting land of contrasting realities.

From the sands of the Thar, the great desert heartland of India, to the foothills of the Himalayas, where the waters from the Gangotri Glacier meld into the lifeblood that is the Ganges, there is both contradiction and a sense of oneness woven into this land and into all those who share it.

Although my time in this land was short, it has left a lasting imprint on my heart and mind. In my heart, I am left with a desire to return to the beauty of the people and the land, as unique and diverse as those entrusted with its future. In my mind, I contemplate a convergence of purpose and passion, within the intricacies of everyday living, for those moments and memories we often overlook, but that will nonetheless inspire the direction of our life's journey.

From this diversity and contrast, we can dare to imagine that we live in a world where all people are unique and singular threads in a patchwork predetermined by our Creator and that the strength of our fabric comes not from the dominance of one thread over another, but instead from a shared destiny and a oneness of purpose. Surely, then, our best dreams will become our most cherished memories!

Note to Self

It's been said for ages in one form or another that music soothes and heals those of us willing to lend a patient ear. It shapes our existence in real ways. Indeed, it was Shakespeare in *Twelfth Night* who wrote, "If music be the food of love, play on!"

As someone who has invested a significant amount of time and resources into listening to music in its various forms throughout my life, I can confidently report that music has shaped my life in measurable and meaningful ways, day by day and note by note.

While listening to music may be a source of entertainment that lifts our spirits and even lightens our load at times, the hidden secret of the melodies and their vocal accompaniment is not so much about what we hear, but more about what we experience in our souls as each note echoes within us.

Each string of the guitar resonates in its own unique way to produce a melody that not only reinforces the tone and timbre of the song but also communicates the thoughts, dreams, and emotions of the musician in a way unlike any other form of communication.

Note by note, the musician reveals the shape of his soul, becoming vulnerable by exposing the soft underbelly of his emotions; in the process, he transforms himself as he pours out his song to eager ears.

Once his song is completed and the last note fades into silence, the musician and his audience are forever changed by the music and the experience that they have shared, each taking from the moment whatever satisfaction, enjoyment, conclusions, or healing may be needed.

The wonder in this process is that it occurs without giving it complete thought; it happens as an autonomous reaction, much like an emotional breath. We have no choice but to respond to the call of music to our souls. We may respond with tears from joyful memories or hidden sorrows, or we may develop an indifference to the tones flooding over us. Still, we will always respond to each note when gathered into a collection of unique or familiar patterns.

Like the music to which we respond, each of us is a unique vibration in the music of life and the song of humankind, as expressed through the shared experiences of our collective journey towards our destiny as a species.

The music of life and love reverberates within us, finding a special place somewhere between heart, mind, and soul.

There, it mixes with our essence under the watchful and loving eyes of the Master Composer.

Our hope and prayer for one another is that the music of life brings only sweet notes to our ears and memories of peace, joy, and love with every awakening.

Winter Upon Us

We wake this morning with the sting of another winter upon our faces. We exhale into the morning air, and we find our lives drifting up and away as if to remind us that we are one beat, one breath, one dawn closer to our destiny.

We jump into our daily routines with a bit of practiced dread, as we would a sleigh on the newly fallen snow, aware of our movement but uncertain of where we are going and oblivious to the call of life passing by us.

We stare into the distance with a sense of wonder and anticipation—another hill to ascend, another valley to cross, more breaths into the chill. The pace of life continues. We get tired even before we step onto new ground.

It has been said that the reason God made the earth round was to keep us from looking too far ahead. We strain our eyes, our minds, and our relationships in a quest for the next mountaintop, forgetting that we willingly travel through the valleys of our lives in between each new victory.

So we ready ourselves for the cold and for the journey ahead. We look around us and capture all the beauty of creation in all that we see. We open our ears to the sounds of life and to the voices of those with whom we share this twisting stone. We capture in our thoughts the best memories of where we have trodden each step on our way towards our destiny.

In trepidation, we command our sleigh to move forward with a nervous smile upon our chilled lips. We venture towards the next mountaintop, knowing that we were not created to be fearful of the climb, but to be assured of our victory; with the knowledge that our future, our destiny, is a matter not of who we are, but of whose we are, and that no winter chill can outlast the warmth of the love we gather within our hearts on our journey.

Our faith is measured by our willingness to trust in our Creator and His plan of good for each of us. It is by that very trust and by our resolve that even during the storm, we can be calm, hopeful, and confident.

While we may have temporarily lost our way, our willingness to trust in Him as our compass and as a Creator who protects us from the turbulence around us allows us to shine as a beacon of faith, leading others to Him and to glorify His name.

Courage...to Love

In his book *Everybody, Always: Becoming Love in a World Full of Setbacks and Difficult People*, the New York Times best-selling author Bob Goff talks about stepping outside of our protected and self-centered personas to become living examples of love in action.

In doing so, we fulfill our spiritual responsibilities by making a positive impact on the lives of others, and we forever change our thinking and the focus for our own lives. Stepping outside of our comfort zones demands both our willingness and the courage to change and to move forward.

For some reason, courage and love are often perceived as unrelated and distinct qualities or personal attributes. In fact, courage is often applied to the tangible aspects and routines of our daily living. At the same time, love is allocated to the realm of feelings, desires, and emotions, far from the reality where courage abides.

We cannot break free from the bonds of our own self-centered mindfulness without taking risks. Stepping outside our comfort zones regarding the love we share with others requires a commitment to loving another unconditionally; that is, without any agenda on our part. When we have an agenda and apply conditions to receiving our love, what we are looking at sharing is not love but a method or program for controlling others.

Giving love unconditionally puts our emotions and even our lives in peril. That is why we need to be courageous when loving others. We have all been down one road or another at times in our lives when we expected people to act or respond in specific ways, and we were disappointed, hurt, or felt betrayed. While it may have been a painful experience for us, we need to examine our conscience and our motives surrounding those experiences to determine if we had an agenda attached to that love and if it was truly offered unconditionally.

Suppose we are authentic in our intentions about sharing our love unconditionally. In that case, we can step forward with courage to truly love another person, knowing that the strength of our spirit and the depth of our faith have the power to lift us above any negative consequences or outcomes that may result from our actions.

1 Corinthians 16:13–14 (New Living Translation Version) cautions us to "be on guard. Stand firm in the faith. Be courageous. Be strong. And do everything with love." Over two thousand years ago, we were guided by Spirit to connect these two different parts of our existence: courage in the corporal world and love in the spiritual. We cannot become everything that we were created to be without developing both aspects of our existence!

Today, Be Gone!

Goodbye, Today! You have brought me neither the happy dreams of a day well lived or the promise of the new dawn.

Your amber rays have cast great shadows of broken promises and of unwilling dreams; still, you call each morning with a message of hope for the day coming upon me, only to dash those hopes when the day is done.

Life demands that we live it, so I am compelled to move forward though you have conspired with my fears to wreak havoc upon my every step and to deny me the joy of anticipating the blessings and the secret pleasures that life has reserved for me.

Though I step forward cautiously, electing to measure my progress along the way with periods of reflection and reassessment, you would have me throw myself at life with recklessness, challenging its passion and purpose, denying me a shared destiny with the others who inhabit this rocky and twisting stone and who, too, awaken to your lies.

Despite your treachery, I will move forward into the light of the new day to confront life on my terms, choosing not to hide in the shadows to await discovery by the approaching dawn, but to venture forward and to confront the ugly wrinkles of life one wrinkle at a time.

While no two steps of my journey will ever be the same, nor will they ever again be walked in quite the same way, where I end up on my journey is determined by the strength of my character and by honing my mettle with the spiritual blade of my faith.

For me, as it is for all the other travelers who awaken to your pretense, our Creator has given us a spirit of strength, not fear. If we are wise and attend to our spiritual growth, then our journey home is one of joy, regardless of the underlying circumstances. Then instead of approaching our destination with uncertainty and counting each step of our journey, we can spend our remaining days counting our blessings and falling asleep each night to the echoes of our victories.

Rain falls on the just, as it does on the unjust. Today might be a bad day simply because bad things sometimes happen in life. We may feel betrayed by life, by circumstances, or by someone around us, or we may feel disappointed. But our Creator has given each of us a spirit of strength and courage to fight our way forward one step at a time until we can finally declare victory.

All of us can feel down at times. With COVID, the state of the economy, a war in Ukraine, the march of time, and all that comes with it, who wouldn't feel down in the dumps occasionally? The critical thing to remember is that while we may not be able to control all that is around us, we have the tools to control what is inside us, and that is something far greater than anything that exists in this world!

So reach out to someone today, tell them how you feel, and ask them how they're doing. We are all unique and singular threads in the fabric of humankind. No one thread is pulled without affecting the others!

Imperfect Practice

Our routines are like rivers in our minds. They flow through us with little or no forethought, like logs riding the outgoing tide.

Awakening one morning early enough to catch the first light of the new day, I clutched my ritual mug of stimulation and fumbled with the remote to find my favorite music to start my day.

With cup in hand, I gently lowered myself into the comfort and familiarity of my favorite chair. I quieted myself for a few minutes of contemplation and praise to the One who parked me on this twisting stone many years ago. There I waited in silence for the whole light of dawn to come upon me.

Experience has taught me that these moments are natural opportunities for reflection, observation, and sometimes profound insight. Occasionally, during this ritual, I find my thoughts drifting towards the people who inhabit the reserved places in my mind, and I ponder what they are thinking, doing, or wanting to communicate to me.

As time passed and the subtle rhythm and tones in the background melded with my thoughts, forming a mantra of unrealized illumination, my thinking and focus were distilled down to the narrowest trickle of relationships. I found myself confronted with the most sobering of questions to ponder concerning what my closest souls and hearts might be thinking or doing at that very moment.

Gathering the courage of my convictions, I reached for my phone, and with a few more quick pokes of my index finger, I dialed up the one individual who I was confident would relate to me on all levels of consciousness and subliminal communication.

Three rings…four rings… Finally, after the fifth ring, my dearest of hearts put an end to my anguish and answered her phone with a cheerful "Hi, honey!" I responded kindly, and we chuckled about how she had just been thinking about me and was preparing to text me her thoughts for the day.

Immediately, I launch into a declaration of enlightenment, sharing the fruits of my morning of reflection and illumination in a download of observations about what she must have been thinking that very same morning as she awoke to the same star under which we both shared the first strains of daylight.

As my dearest began to unravel her thoughts upon my half-willing ears, I began to wrestle with the reality of her words. I quickly found myself forming a new observation and a very different realization: my complete lack of understanding of what she had been thinking about and how, or even if, it might relate to me. I quickly found myself in a practiced ritual of silent listening and occasional short, confirming responses, and I realized that what I had romantically and willingly fashioned into a symbiotic soliloquy of shared consciousness was, in reality, quite different.

We finished our volley of half-awake observations and bid each other mutual goodbyes, promising to connect again later in the day. I settled myself again in my favorite chair and reached for my coffee mug, taking comfort in the familiarity and warmth of its contents. I allowed myself to exhale deeply and tilted my head upward, closing my eyes for a moment of reflection.

In that silence, I realized how vulnerable we all are to our routines and expectations. It occurred to me as well that our practiced patterns of thinking and actions apply not only to those things that we correctly assume about the world around us and the people who share it with us, but also to those thoughts, assumptions, and attitudes where we fall short.

We are, at our core, creatures of habit. Good and bad. Our hope is anchored in the strength of our faith and our spiritual growth. In this growth, we experience a new awakening of our consciousness, one that transcends our human frailties and opens up more opportunities for us to broaden our thinking beyond the space we occupy and the patterned thinking and actions that come so easily to us.

Though we may not yet have arrived at the point that destiny has assigned to us, we have traveled far, and we are weary of the journey. We are, after all, little more than creamy swirls in the tepid blackness of reality!

For the Love of Jessie

A Desert Love Story

It had been some time since I last heard anything about Jessie—no letters, no phone calls, no postcards, nothing at all. I hadn't heard anything for such a long time that I often wondered if she was real or if my memories of her were nothing more than fantasies conjured up to help smooth out the bumpy road down which my life seemed to turn all too frequently.

I was quick to recall our chance meeting from so many years ago. I returned to the beauty and wonder of the desert Southwest, a part of the country that had become a collection of cherished memories and grand images of endless blue skies, ancient mountain peaks, and blistering deserts spotted with outcroppings of saguaro, organ cactus, and desert sage.

My business travel has allowed me the opportunity to visit many interesting places over the years, but the Sonoran Desert held a special magic for me. Though I was inspired by the sheer beauty of the high desert and its cascade of sights, smells, and the naked awe that it created within me, it was the silent breeze of the desert wind that filled my senses with passion and a reverence for life. It was a spiritual awakening for me, something I came to refer to as "the breath of God."

Those early visits to the desert and the surrounding mountains brought to life for me the many books I had read about the enchantment and power found in this land. It also provided me a few reference points for my addiction to the Tony Hillerman series of Navajo Nation police stories, all of which I eagerly consumed as quickly as they were released. Visions and sounds of Window Rock, Ship Rock, the Salt River, and the *Diné Bahane'* (Navajo creation story also known as *Story of the People*) all brought me closer to thinking of this part of the country as my second home.

Several years earlier, I was with a client who was interested in seeing some of the work that my company was doing at our manufacturing facility in the hills just north of Phoenix. Usually, it would have been a typically quick in-and-out visit that would have me heading home to Connecticut a day or two after my arrival. But, this time, I decided to stay on a few days longer to explore the area and to enjoy the warmth of the Arizona sunshine in early April. It was in that extra time, hiking the trails up and around Camelback Mountain, where I first encountered Jessie.

Like me, Jessie was out enjoying the beauty of the high desert one morning, stopping to examine a flowering cactus in the predawn stillness and standing in silence long enough to gather the bits of sights, sounds, and smells that would combine somewhere between heart and mind as a special moment and a lasting memory. She and I crossed paths a few times as we both worked our way up and down the terrain leading to the observation deck that awaited both of us atop the mountain.

As I took my final few steps up to the landing where the observation deck was located, I could see in the distance that Jessie had already arrived there. Though I was winded from the climb, Jessie appeared unaffected. Later, I would learn that she was a regular visitor to this spot on the mountain; her frequent walks contributed to her athletic prowess and overall fitness, which was visible in her taut and beautifully shaped body.

There on the observation deck, we both stood in silence and awe as we looked out over the initial stretch of desert to the sprawling shadows and distant sounds of the city as the desert rolled out below us into the distant mountains to the south. We looked at each other in silence; both of us knew that something special was happening. That was the beginning of a relationship and a friendship unlike any I had ever experienced up to that time in my life, and it remains so to this day.

But now, as I set off on my adventure around the Thanksgiving holiday, I couldn't help but wonder if my journey would mark the beginning of another direction in my life. Would it signal the start of a renewed friendship? Would this be my chance to pump some life into a heart smitten by love? Or would this be a few days of frustration in the desert, a pawn in Jessie's cruel Sonoran charade?

Living out there in her corner of the desert, amid the sand and the sage, Jessie hid from the blistering sun during the day and then fell asleep each night beneath a twinkling sea of distant points of light. She lived out her days in her singular way, choosing the solitude of her desert landscape over the weary pace of life in the city, putting behind her the people and disappointments of long ago, and taking only what she needed from the land and from the kind souls who had taken it upon themselves to adopt Jessie into their family, a bond not of blood but of simple love and mutual respect.

More than once before, I had fallen victim to the charms of this desert princess. It was so many years ago when that dream last ended. But the memory of her scent, those bright eyes, and the silky glow of her curls still captivated my imagination and curiosity about what might have been. Back in those days, our lives were busy with every sort of distraction. My business trips provided ample opportunities to experience what life with Jessie would be like. Still, other matters and priorities diverted our attention, which we would have preferred to share if we had been given ample time and opportunity.

It seemed that neither of us was willing to spend the time or effort to truly get to know one another. We settled instead for infrequent glimpses of what could have been; if only we could slow down our lives just enough to connect in a way that was something more than superficial, more than occasional, maybe then we could make it work. But fate had determined that we go our separate ways, and so we turned our attentions to more pressing matters and other people in our lives, putting the what-ifs on the back burners of our memories.

But now, after so many years and countless recollections, I found myself quite unexpectedly driving up the long series of switchbacks and cactus outcroppings that led to Jessie's place in the high desert, where she seemed happiest and willing to let the years spin on in quiet solitude and reflection. What led me to call on her? Why did I care? Would spending these days together mean something more than renewing a friendship? Would this be another beginning for us or just a revisit to the dead ends to which we had grown accustomed so many times over the years?

As my rental car pulled itself up over the ridge at the top of the dirt driveway leading to Jessie's front porch, I could see a familiar face in the shadows just beyond the screen door. My heart began to race, and my palms grew moist as I momentarily flashed back to another time when I would eagerly anticipate these high-desert rendezvous, knowing the joy, the playful spirit, and the quiet times that we both found intoxicating. Excitement, uncertainty, regret—all these emotions seemed to flow through my body as I pulled up to the front porch, put the car in park, and set the parking brake. Before I could prepare myself, Jessie had already sprinted to my rental car and poked her head into my driver's window, welcoming my arrival with the sparkling eyes and broad smile that had long ago etched themselves into my memory.

As I stood to greet her properly, I could see that she had kept herself fit, trim, and very athletic. No doubt she maintained her well-practiced routines of morning walks, hikes through the high desert, and occasional runs. Topping off her athletic frame were her bright eyes, broad smile, and the same soft red curls and shiny hair that I remembered from so many years earlier. I held myself in check, yearning to lose myself in those silky curls once again and playfully roll around with her on the living room floor or the bed, as we had done in the past, and teasingly enjoy the simple pleasures of unspoken moments between friends.

I settled into my guest room, put away a few clothes, made myself more presentable, and met up with Jessie in front of the fireplace at the foot of the old high-back wing chair, which I had come to know as a favorite spot for Jessie to warm herself and to share the quieter moments. Much of our past was filled with moments like these, when memories, emotions, a glass of wine, and unspoken desires replaced the need for words. The crackling fire, the warming glow, and the dancing reflections in Jessie's dark eyes communicated everything I needed to know.

The evening came upon us as the roar of the fire turned into a rhythmic series of pops and hisses that welcomed the more intimate hours of the evening as we found ourselves once again curled up together by the hearth, on the oval rug I had purchased in Santa Fe many years earlier as a gift for Jessie. With a pillow under our heads, wine completed, and Jessie's head resting peacefully on my shoulder, I wrapped my arms around her, enjoying the warmth of her body, letting my fingers playfully delight in her curls. We were back to a place where we both felt safe, comfortable, trusting, and familiar.

As the clock on Jessie's fireplace mantel squeezed out the last few hours of the day, we each took turns dozing in front of the dying embers, watching each other, studying the curves in each other's faces, and cuddling closer as the warmth of the fire became a memory.

Then, in a shared moment of renewal, we both looked at each other, eyes wide open, face-to-face, silent in our words, but communicating so much to one another. Slowly, I rolled over onto my back and gently embraced Jessie, pulling her softly over me. She willingly assumed a familiar position as she made herself comfortable on top of my outstretched frame. The reflections and excitement of the past were once again being realized. We both knew it, and we enjoyed losing ourselves in the moment.

The following morning, I awoke to Jessie's kiss as she plopped down beside me in bed. It was a new day and time to create fresh adventures and revisit familiar ones. As I readied myself, I kept thinking of the night before and how much I had missed Jessie and those things that we shared in the fire's afterglow. It was equally comforting to know that my memories from similar nights and reunions had not been distorted…or worse, imagined. Those memories were real, as real as the sparkle in Jessie's eyes and the affection she poured out with such gentleness and fullness.

We spent the day walking the trails up and down Camelback Mountain, listening to the quiet that can only be found in the desert, sniffing the piñons and scrub pines that dotted the landscape as we made our way back to Jessie's house. The day had come to an end; now, I needed to return to my schedule of stops and appointments, taking with me the memories of this happy reunion of old friends and leaving behind the thoughts, desires, and dreams of what might come again.

It was time to leave. I said goodbye and hoped to make a clean getaway before I became a victim of emotions and regrets. I climbed back into my rental car, turned the key in the ignition, and adjusted my rearview mirror. In the mirror, I could see Jessie standing on the front porch, quiet and looking very distant.

As I began the drive down the long dirt road from the house to the highway, I glanced back in the rearview mirror and saw Jessie leap from the porch and sprint towards me. Almost instantly, she was at my driver's window to collect one more goodbye. I grabbed at her red curls one last time as Jessie drowned me with kisses on my lips, my ears, and all over my face. Then, as quickly as she had sprinted over to my window, she turned away and ran back to her spot on the front porch.

As I pulled away, I could see Jessie position herself in front of the screen door, resigned to my departure. Dropping herself to the floor, her eyes closed, her face showed the sadness of the moment and the uncertainty of what the future would bring. She gathered herself once again, dropping her head between her front paws, quieting her wagging tail. She fixed her eyes on my vehicle one last time as I headed out towards the road, anticipating once again my return and knowing, as I did, that in the magic and wonder of the desert, true love and friendship transcend time, distance, and even species. God has been gracious!

A Calling of Echoes

The Desert Southwest has always intrigued me. The stark contrasts between the ragged peaks of the high desert, the dried riverbeds filled with tumbleweeds and sage, the deafening silence leaving only the windy wisps of creation, all envelop me in a personalized spirituality.

Over many years of dancing to the music of life, the desert has been a faithful and welcome companion whose company I have sought during the twists and turns of my life's journey. Each visit, each memory, a renewal.

Like the sunlit peaks in the distance and the shadowy mesas behind us, life returns our memories, one by one, so that we may examine and experience again the thoughts, words, and actions we have sent out as clarions announcing our existence.

If we choose to send love into the universe, it too will return to us as a distant echo. Love seeks out the faintest strains of sunlight in the deepest recesses of our being, no matter how deep the darkness or how firm the grasp of night.

Love builds its momentum through the kindness of thoughts turned to actions, and it settles into the most distant corners of our hearts as if echoes returning home, whispering into our being the reassuring melody of oneness.

For true love endures both the highest highs and the lowest lows with a grace and quiet confidence urging us to keep on believing, to go on loving, and to never stop dreaming, together.

Into the Sublime

If I had to choose how to live each new day, I would choose to see sunshine every step of the way.

I would watch the sun welcomed into grey morning skies and listen more closely to birds on the fly.

I would think of my children, their lives now afar, of things that they said when they wished on a star.

I would ponder the smiles of grandsons so bright, of their visions and dreams as they enter the night.

I would sing a new song every day of the week and summon my smile every day to repeat.

I would conjure up love—simple, timeless, and true. I would give in to passion and the things lovers do.

I would end my day softly in the arms of my love, whisper prayers of thanksgiving to the One up above.

I would fall asleep grateful for having the time to ask you once again my love, "Dance with me into the sublime?"

Nate's Way

November skies were cold and clear the day good fortune left you here. To start your life with eyes so blue, a tender cry, and dimples too!

Who is this child, this special boy? Hearts filled to the brim with love and joy. Wrapped up tight in swaddling clothes, our dreams of happiness are now yours to know.

For now, our anxious minds do rest, but soon we shall endure the test.

You'll stretch your arms to welcome life, the path you'll choose, the battles you'll fight.

Your days to print upon our hearts, each victory cherished from the start. Till once again you find your way home to light up our hearts, never more to roam.

A Field of Dreams

Recently, I've spent a lot of my spare time reading about some of the latest discoveries and theories in the field of particle physics. One of the most controversial of these theories is known as quantum field theory.

Mercifully, even if I could, I will not attempt to explain the theory. However, the abbreviated explanation is that all of creation—including stars, planets, and people—is composed of countless different "fields" that move and vibrate in various ways to create the perception of particles, people, and planets. It's a pretty cool theory. I like to think of it as the physicists' Field of Dreams.

Moving now to simpler concepts, I recall being in the heart of my seventh-grade year at Saint Rita's School in Hamden, Connecticut. At that point in my life, my field was much more tangible; it was the baseball diamond at my elementary school, and my dream was to play on a baseball team. The lure of Little League baseball gripped me as well as my friends with equal gravity and expectation. As they geared up for the thrill of the game, I decided to join the ranks, my sights set on becoming a pitcher.

Daily driveway practices became my routine, and I gave my all on tryout day, both on the pitcher's mound and at bat. Despite finding some success as a pitcher, my hitting skills were abysmal, and disappointment washed over me as I learned I hadn't made the team.

Enter my dad, perceptive to my disappointment. In the days that followed, my dad and I attended team practices even though I had failed to make the team. He had a plan!

One evening, as we watched from behind home plate when team practice was ending, my dad spotted Father McDonald, the priest overseeing school sports. My dad sprang up from the bleachers where we were sitting and ran over to where Father McDonald was talking with the head coach.

To my horror, my dad went about introducing himself to both Father McDonald and the head coach, occasionally turning his head towards where I was sitting as he spoke with them. With calm and finesse, my dad passionately detailed my hard work and dashed hopes of making the team.

Father McDonald, a compassionate soul but not wanting to challenge the head coach's decision overtly, huddled with the coach, who bluntly stated to the horror of my ears and my ego, "But, Father, he can't hit the ball. He stinks."

After a short period of deliberation, Father McDonald called my dad and me over. He put his hand on my shoulder and bent over to speak with me face-to-face. With a smile and a tone of excitement in his voice, he declared, "We've got room on the team for you!"

Ecstatic, I thanked the priest, and we headed home.

That season, I may have confirmed the coach's assessment—I stunk, and hitting eluded me. Yet I relished being part of something that brought joy to my friends and me. Their camaraderie transcended my struggles with baseball, proving that being part of the team mattered more than my hitting woes. My friends never judged me, and I cherished the happiness derived from shared excitement, even if I couldn't hit the ball.

Looking back at that time with the benefit of hindsight and many years of living, I can see that everyone involved in my baseball experience was right. My dad was right, Father McDonald was right, and the coach was right; I did stink! But in the end, I got what I needed: a feeling of being included, of being a part of something bigger and greater than myself.

Each of us has experienced a moment of disentanglement—a time when we feel detached from the world and the people around us, watching from the sidelines as life passes us by. Hopes, dreams, and expectations may seem overly ambitious during these periods of self-imposed solitude and reflection. Still, we often forget that with each experience, with each step in our life journey, we learn something about ourselves and about how each of us is connected.

Like the mind-bending theories of quantum entanglement, in which each event or action affecting one particle affects all others, regardless of the distance between them, we are all singular and unique threads in the fabric of humankind; anything that affects one thread pulls at all the others.

Batter up!

The Circle Game

The spinning rock upon which we all live makes its way effortlessly around our star on a predictable path and has done so for countless billions of years.

Yet science teaches us that our distance from the sun, the tilt of our planet, as well as its rotational speed, are constantly changing. In fact, even our sun will change over time to swell in size and eventually devour our very insignificant planet sometime in the very distant future.

The dilemma for all of us in this learning process is that, even as we experience living in measured moments, with expected outcomes and neatly stored memories, everything around us constantly changes, including us.

The appearance of order in our universe and our lives is an illusion. We live in a constant state of chaos. Everything we have learned since our very first breath of our changing atmosphere continues to be redefined, reshaped, and repositioned for our future use and understanding as we step forward on our individual journey through life.

Each of us then reacts to the changes around us and within us in a never-ending dance with chaos as we bump into one another like spinning tops on a table. Our predictability within our own daily rituals changes; so too does the predictability of those with whom we share our journey.

Finding patterns in the chaos allows us, at any point on our journey through life, to grasp insights into living that have immediate value to us as long as we understand that what we learn today, like us, will someday vanish and be recycled in the endless game we now play.

A Matter of Perspective

In the vast cosmic dance of time and space, a quest for meaning, the human race. From dawn's first light to twilight's embrace, we ponder the essence; the purpose we chase. What lies beyond this mortal shore? A riddle as old as existence's core. In nature's symphony, we yearn to explore the elusive answer forevermore.

Is life a fleeting breath, a weary sigh? A mere interlude before we say goodbye. Or is it a tapestry, colors that fly, threads woven together as the moments pass by? In the gentle whispers of a summer breeze, or the roaring waves of mighty seas, in the laughter of children, their innocent ease, we catch a glimpse of the echoes of life's mysteries.

For life's true meaning lies not in a name, nor material wealth or transient fame. It blooms in compassion, in love's sacred flame, in kind acts and virtues, our souls to reclaim. So embrace the beauty of each fleeting day and find solace in moments that silently pass. Seek truth in the stars as they eternally play, and let gratitude guide your heart on the way.

For when our journey's complete and the shadows descend, the true meaning of life will be found in the end, in the echoes of hearts healed by love, and in the blessings we've shared, our gifts from above.

In thanksgiving and grace, our spirits are humbled; under the light of brotherhood, we shall not stumble; instead, we can dance, no regrets, no reason for sorrow, just joy, peace, and wonder as we look towards tomorrow.

So let us dance in harmony with all the unknowns, with open hearts and spirits forever grown, embracing the wonders life has shown, for in the meaning we seek, we are never alone!

Calls to the Heart

A gift lies waiting at my bed's cold foot—a moment, a memory, a tender shoot. A heart, both strong and true, that yearns to love and be loved this Valentine's anew.

But blinded eyes, a vision preconceived, keep treasures hidden. I long believed that love must come in some specific guise, and so I missed the truth behind your eyes.

I sought a shadow, undefined and vast, while joy stood waiting, built to last. I walked alone, though willing hands were near, and whispered hopes I held so very dear.

Afraid to show the light that burned within, the yearning deep, the love I longed to win. Yet on this path, our destinies entwine, a shared road forward, yours and also mine.

So let me see now, eyes opened wide, the beauty, the truth that life has set aside. No longer searching for a phantom's call, but recognizing love, embracing all.

This special day, I give thanks and pray that love's blessing I'll see today. A heart to cherish and a hand to hold, a love returned, a story to unfold.

Find Your Way

Whisper's Poem

In the dawning light of a new year's grace, may your steps find paths of wonder to embrace. Discoveries that shimmer, yet unseen; a tapestry of life, vibrant and keen.

Let kindness blossom in your gentle soul, overflowing freely and making others whole—hope, a beacon, guiding your every stride; love's tender embrace, where hearts confide.

In the simplest pleasures, find pure delight—the sun's warm kiss, the stars in the night. Share this joy with open hands and heart, a symphony of souls, a work of art!

With each step forward, destiny unfolds; a journey of purpose, stories yet untold. Dance with a happy heart, light and free; embrace the sublime, your spirit's decree.

May this year be a canvas bright and true, where dreams take flight and hopes are renewed. In the whispers in the wheatfield, find your way in the light of new beginnings, forever and today!

Reflections

As the year exhales its final breath, relinquishing the last hours of its fading light, I stand once more on the shores of thought, watching the waves of memory crash and recede.

The days have been measured, the minutes lost, yet the echoes linger, soft and profound, whispering truths of struggle and solace, of light sought and shadows embraced.

I have witnessed the cycle of life unfold, family and friends drawn to the eternal shoreline, each one a wave, unique in rhythm and form, leaving their essence upon the sands of time. They linger, a gift to those of us waiting, teaching us to honor the tide, to stand in awe of its mystery, and to cherish the moments it lends us.

Once more, I confront the vast questions: What is the purpose? What is the connection? Does the soul outlast the stars? Seventy-five orbits around the sun have left me with fewer answers, and yet, in the uncertainties, I find a curious kind of peace—a knowing that not knowing is enough.

Tomorrow, should it arrive, I will rise like the morning sun, my mind perhaps fogged with age, yet steady in its ritual, guided by the rhythm of the waves. I will walk alongside the spirits of those who have already come ashore and ponder their dwelling place—is it a realm of purpose or an eternal void?

Yet in this pondering, a truth emerges: immortality is not the key to life's meaning. To live a life of service—of kindness, joy, and quiet love—is to find the essence of existence. Every second, every fleeting breath holds its sacred worth.

As the first light of a new day unfolds into the present, I carry this wisdom with me. Life is enough. It is a fleeting spark in the vast darkness, a chance to leave our trace upon the shore and revel in the beauty of the journey!

Poor Me!

A Thanksgiving Day Lament

Poor me, I started my Christmas shopping today… Black Friday sales, you know!

Poor me, I began wrapping a few Christmas presents today, and I emptied the refrigerator of the leftover Thanksgiving turkey, stuffed cabbage, and chocolate pie. I needed to make room in preparation for the upcoming Christmas dinner with friends and family.

Poor me, I'll be driving to New York over the holidays to dine with my son and his beautiful wife and to see my grandsons. Traffic will be awful!

Poor me, I'll be cooking all morning on Christmas Day and most of Christmas Eve. Can you believe it? Hopefully, we will have time for a cozy dinner at our favorite Italian bistro after the Christmas Eve candlelight service. I hope the sermon doesn't go too long!

Poor me, I'll need to get an early start on Christmas morning so that I can prepare the turkey and prime rib in time for Christmas dinner. I wish that I had a double oven.

Poor me, I'll be slicing potatoes for the au gratin and mixing the green beans for the casserole, and I'll probably forget to chill the cranberry sauce, not to mention burn the dinner rolls.

Poor me, I just spent a bunch of money on wine, Champagne, and vodka (Polish, of course) for the Christmas Day merriment. I hope to have time to look at the new Lexus this weekend; there doesn't seem to be enough hours in the day!

Poor me, I was interrupted several times yesterday by friends and family who called to wish me holiday cheers for the upcoming Christmas and New Year's celebrations. Sometimes it's overwhelming, and silence is welcome.

Poor me, I went down to my breakfast spot earlier today, and I sat next to a homeless man at the breakfast counter; he walked with a cane, he wore old clothes and was unshaven, he didn't leave a tip for the server, but he said that he would make up for it the next time he came in there.

Poor me, I finished my chores early today and stopped by the pub for a beer and some conversation. I felt a little lonely because I sat by myself and surfed the internet with my new iPad, looking for more holiday bargains, but none were left to scratch off my Christmas gift list.

Poor me, I finished all of my post-Thanksgiving activities, food shopping, and holiday planning. I gassed up my Jeep after running it through the car wash, then headed home to collapse into my favorite chair in front of my fireplace to finish the day with a Bach sonata and a sip of Irish whiskey.

Poor me, as I reflected on my day, I realized that my honest lament was that I had missed an opportunity to buy breakfast for a homeless person, encourage him, or take him shopping for a new item of clothing.

Poor me, I missed the opportunity to get him a haircut. I missed the chance to ask him his name, to let him know that I care about him. Poor me indeed!

Autumn's Embrace

A canvas painted in gold and red as leaves descend in a graceful ballet, their freedom spreading across the land. The season shifts, and magic fills the air as nature's beauty takes us by surprise.

A time for gathering, for friends and kin, where laughter echoes and warmth begins. The football roars, the feast is spread with care as autumn's blessings fill the air.

From summer's heat, our minds, to chill as twilight's hues paint the evening sky. The sun's last rays, a fading golden light, as nature's palette takes a wondrous flight.

The trees stand bare, like lovers unashamed, their branches exposed, their secrets unclaimed. Each falling leaf, a dancer's intricate art, as autumn's winds play their enchanting part.

A time of death, or transformation's grace, as memories fade or leave their trace. Reflection's hour, a moment to prepare for what lies ahead, beyond despair.

All endings are beginnings, so they say, a truth revealed in life's unfolding play. Through change, we're shaped, our paths defined as joy and sorrow intertwine.

Unique threads woven in life's tapestry, a shared experience for all to see. Though our paths are diverse, a common light within, a guiding star through the din of darkness.

We choose our seeds to plant or let them fall in rocky ground or fertile soil. The choice is ours; the outcome is yet to be seen—a journey's end or a new beginning.

Each wave arrives with a unique destiny, each snowflake's beauty wild and free—diversity's dance a constant in our sight, a reminder of creation's infinite light.

In the Nick of Time

I once heard that it only takes twelve minutes out of an entire day for someone to determine whether their day was good or bad.

According to the theory, only twelve minutes of negative input, activity, or otherwise-unpleasant experiences in a given day can produce a negative attitude about whether the day was good or bad.

Perhaps even more interesting is that it didn't matter whether the adverse reaction was the result of a series of unrelated events during the day, adding up to twelve minutes, or if it was the product of a single twelve-minute blast of negative disruption. The result was the same; twelve minutes of negative experience produced the same conclusion about that day.

Allowing ourselves to be influenced so profoundly by such a small slice of daily living seems to devalue most of our thoughts, breaths, and other moments in our day, or, for that matter, in our lives.

While twelve minutes of disruption may seem too short an interval on which to shape our attitude of that day, it is certain that just one moment of brokenheartedness colors our day as profoundly as the cream in our morning coffee, changing the tone and texture, and influencing our ability to enjoy the present fully.

Fortunately, our Creator placed within us a spirit of strength and endurance to overcome the moments of disruption, anger, and disappointment.

Whether it be a span of minutes or months, our hope is in His promise to us that, no matter what it is, we have within us all that it takes to endure for however long it may be and to finish each day with a smile, looking forward to the new dawn with grateful thanksgiving and anticipation…coffee cup in hand!

Fear, Uncertainty, and Doubt

Part 1—The Call

The unique benefits of freedom and independence, won so often with the sacrifice and toil of the innocent, can never be taken for granted.

Like all things of truth and value in our lives, whether it be in America, in India, or in some small and insignificant speck of land in the middle of the ocean, our freedom and independence is eternally linked to our respect for each other and our recognition that the things we share of mind, matter, and spirit are far greater than those forces that would drive us apart from one another!

Freedom is a complex tapestry woven with threads of history, bravery, and resilience. Each strand tells a tale of battles fought and sacrifices made, reminding us that the liberties we enjoy today are the fruits of immense struggle and perseverance. Independence is not merely a political state; it's a state of being, a cherished condition in which individuals possess the liberty to think, express, and live without the constraints imposed by oppression and tyranny.

As we reflect on the significance of freedom, it becomes clear that independence is more than a national celebration. It is a daily commitment to uphold the values of justice, equality, and fraternity. It is in the moments of everyday life—when we choose to speak out against injustice, extend a hand to our neighbors, and cherish the diversity that enriches our communities—that the true essence of freedom is realized.

Moreover, the pursuit of freedom is an ongoing journey. It demands vigilance and active participation from each of us to protect and nurture it. In a world where divisions can be deepened by intolerance and misunderstanding, it is crucial to remember that our shared humanity binds us together more strongly than any differences. The freedoms we cherish thrive in an environment where respect and empathy flourish.

To truly honor the sacrifices made for our independence, we must foster a culture of inclusivity and mutual respect. This involves listening to diverse perspectives, engaging in meaningful dialogue, and embracing the richness that comes from our varied backgrounds and experiences. By doing so, we create a society that not only values freedom but also understands its responsibilities.

So as we celebrate our independence, let us do so with gratitude for the past and a resolute commitment to the future. Let us cherish the freedoms we enjoy and strive to ensure that they are preserved and passed on to future generations. With a spirit of unity and a heart full of hope, we can continue to build a world in which freedom and independence are the cornerstones of our shared existence.

Happy Fourth of July!

Fear, Uncertainty, and Doubt

Part 2—The Hope

We live in an uncertain world, perhaps even more so today than ever before. However, human existence has been on an uncertain and unstable path for thousands of years. Recorded history is littered with blood, sweat, and tears resulting from the uncertainties and disruptions that have plagued the world. Over this vast amount of human history, there have been tyrants, saints, and fools, as well as great suffering and great awakening.

We are human; as such, we cannot help but think about the past—our mistakes, poor decisions, failures, and so on. Additionally, as human beings, we are burdened with worries about tomorrow, our children and grandchildren, and the state of our world.

The future is indeed uncertain, but what we can rely on in this uncertain future is the love of our Creator and His plan of good for us. These are times that test our faith. Do we give in to the fears of uncertainty, or do we rely on our faith to lead us through whatever the future turns out to be?

Part of being human is the need to control the people and things around us; we can become frustrated, fearful, and depressed when we realize that we only have control over what we think, do, and how we react to the people and events in our lives. If we can learn to let go of control just enough to entrust our worries and expectations to a higher power, then we can free ourselves to enjoy life, no matter what is happening around us.

This is not disconnecting from the reality of day-to-day living, nor is it running away from making the tough decisions in our lives. It is a conscious choice to focus on the good that is all around us and to surrender our fears and uncertainties to a power and a presence greater than any challenge we may face in life.

We need to remind ourselves that we are only visitors in this world; we are not of it. We are spiritual beings who are all a part of something bigger and greater than any issue, problem, or circumstance of life. It's not about the size or number of issues we may be experiencing; it's about the size of our Creator and the depth of our faith!

Summer Awakening

Passion and sensitivity are two different faces of the same coin. They demand our attention to the nuances of life as we journey into the unknown of tomorrow. They are both prize and payment for committing to a life in search of meaning, connection, and destiny.

We don't all need to walk the Great Wall of China to find passion and experience life's sensitivities. They are often found within an arm's reach of us, crouching within the wrinkles of everyday living.

A great cup of coffee and a sunrise, a cocktail shared in the beauty of companionship, feet in the warm beach sand, a special meal, a golden sunset, a secret place to enjoy an autumn afternoon, the hugs and laughter of our grandchildren—if we can't find passion and sensitivity in these things, then we surely won't find them in some exotic destination.

Embrace the here and now!

Risk Management

Pour out gentleness, kindness, peace, self-control, patience, goodness, joy, faithfulness, and love, for these are all the Fruits of the Spirit, and they are highly prized.

Seek not intelligence, but enlightenment. Do not be consumed with endless questions and a search for truth, but rather be eager to apply what you already know for the benefit of those around you.

Deliver all that you are and what you have with class, confidence, and a sense of humility. Do not fear being lonely, for you are created to fit beautifully into the patchwork of many quilts.

While there is much risk in love, great joy is found when it is realized. Taking risks with one's love can lead to disappointment and heartache, but the same courage it takes to step forward in faith and love someone will sustain you, no matter what the outcome.

Take the risk and dare to love again.

Compelling Transition

The first evidence of impending fall is a magical moment. Once again, we ready ourselves to pay homage to the four horsemen of the autumn apocalypse: family, friends, food, and football. We prepare ourselves for the change in weather, dragging forward our battle attire from the depths of its summer hiatus and putting away one set of tools in exchange for those more appropriately suited to the tasks of the new season.

Half dead from the heat of the departing summer solstice, our minds begin to chill, as does the evening air. We drink in the last few rays of the retreating summer sun and watch the sky above our heads ready itself for a new palette of color splashed over the outstretched branches as the trees prepare to reveal their naked forms like unashamed and exuberant lovers.

Every falling leaf performs its own perfectly choreographed dance as the autumn winds set it free from its summer bondage and coax it towards its private destiny as if it were a dancer being delivered to a waiting audience. In time, its brothers and sisters will follow, providing a clear view of the sky above and blanketing our once-peaceful walks with the crackling of summer memories beneath our feet.

For some, the change of season is a sign of death or transformation, the passing of what was, of experiences and memories lived and now stored for eternity, or for however long it is that our aging memories will allow. For others, it is a time of reflection and preparation for what lies ahead. In truth, it is a bit of both.

It has been said that "all endings are beginnings; we just don't know it at the time." To all but the most cynical and unshakingly stubborn of minds, there is evidence of this truth in our very lives, or at least in the witnessed lives of others.

Whether it occurs in the form of a job change, a move to a new home, the loss of a relationship, or the death of someone important to us, we have all experienced either pain, confusion, excitement, or joy when we transition from what was to what is now.

There are many commonalities and shared threads that run through our lives. Each of us uniquely defines the color and weight of those threads, but they are all woven into a cloth shared by all. We may sometimes wonder how it is that the uniqueness of threads, the repeating patterns of our daily lives, and the oneness and commonality of our creation can allow for such a variety of outcomes in our lives, for such diversity of life.

We need to remind ourselves that while our Creator has planted seeds of greatness within each of us, he has also given us the free will to decide how to use those seeds. Whether we squander them by casting the seeds onto rocky ground during thorny patches of our lives, or we choose to nurture them in the fertile soils of faith, goodness, and love, the choice and the outcomes belong to us.

Every arrival in the endless procession of waves is celebrated when each finds its place and time to come ashore. Every delicate snowflake wears its face among the many with whom it gathers. Our world and all life within it constantly remind us of the diversity of creation in all its forms.

While each of us is divinely made and uniquely singular, and we reflect our light in a way unique to our being, we also shine from within with a common light imbued by our Creator—a light that permits the discovery of our unique paths in life and one that guides us home, an ever-present beacon through the uncertain nights and the stormy days of our journey.

On the Right Path

Autumn holds a grip on my heart. Each year, as the palette of colors changes across the broad hills and valleys, I often find myself crunching leaves beneath my steps and questioning my current path down the road on which I am currently traveling.

Life requires that we live it to the fullest extent possible, so we are compelled to move forward on our journey. The pace of our steps, how we move forward, and the direction we take are of our own choosing.

We may decide to step forward cautiously, electing to measure our progress along the way with periods of reflection and reassessment, or we may throw ourselves at life with recklessness and a sense of destiny.

Whether we choose to move forward into the light of each new day and confront life on our own terms, or hide in the shadows and wait to be discovered by life, we are pulled forward on our journey, one day, one step at a time.

We may venture forward with eyes closed to obscure the ugly wrinkles of life, or perhaps we choose to greet each new day with eyes wide open, hoping to take in every bit of light from the new dawn and measure our journey in tiny slices so that we can squeeze out every unborn memory.

Either way, no two steps of our journey through life will ever be the same, nor will they ever again be walked in quite the same way. We are unique creations. Where we end up on our journey is determined by the strength of our character and the direction we choose with each step forward as we make our way home.

E
F P
F O Z
E O E D
D E C F D
L B C O F D
P L P O F Z D
B O D F O D Z Z

E 3 O 6 7 8 9 9 O

Fatal Vision

Sometimes in life, beauty, truth, and destiny stare us in the face, unrecognized, until we open our eyes fully to see what God, in His wisdom and love, has already planned for us.

We bring life to that plan, and we honor Him by unwrapping those gifts and celebrating them with every sunrise, then carefully putting them away each evening, only to be reopened and shared again the next day.

Often, we are blinded to our blessings and don't see the unopened gifts at the foot of our bed, waiting to be discovered each morning, or we have a predetermined vision or expectation of what gift awaits us. As a result, we fix our eyes on other things and look past the joy and possibilities already within our reach.

It's been said that the reason why God made the earth round was so that we cannot see too far down the road. Perhaps a little nearsightedness is a good thing!

Absolute Zeros

In science, the term "absolute zero" is used to describe the temperature at which, in theory, all molecular activity ceases. At approximately minus 460 degrees Fahrenheit, things don't behave the way that we think they should.

While the molecular behavior changes, the basic makeup and potential of this frigid species of matter remain intact. Perhaps there is a parallel between the workings of our physical world and those of our spiritual existence.

Throughout our long journey from unenlightened creatures of darkness to self-directed and self-actualizing beings of conscience, we have established our own rules for social interactions, responsibilities, and expectations in our day-to-day lives.

We have also developed a "roll your own" attitude towards social behaviors and the underlying principles of decency, morality, and common courtesy.

At times, it seems as if we have rewritten history and religious teaching, and Moses came down from the mountain with ten suggestions instead of commandments. Where have the moral absolutes in our world gone?

Perhaps we can learn something more from the physical world around us and apply it to our search for goodness, decency, and the truth about our existence.

Like the frozen specks of matter held in the icy void, our hearts have been chilled to the point that we no longer behave in the way our Creator intended.

But, just as in the physical world around us, where the tiniest spark of energy transforms everything, our abiding faith in His plan of good for us liberates our hearts from frozen stillness and enables each of us to move to a higher level of existence and morality. We have been so empowered.

Strokes of Genius

The value of a great painting isn't found in the sum of brushstrokes, paint, or canvas; its value is given by its creator.

In the same manner, our value as individuals isn't found solely in the sum of our words, actions, possessions, or accomplishments; our Creator instills our value.

Each word that we speak, every action we take, every kindness shown or withheld has the potential to increase or decrease our joy and the benefits from the value already given to us.

We are forever spiritual painters; through our faith, poured out as actions, we have the opportunity each day to empty our good onto all with whom we meet!

Connected Starlight

The term "cosmic consciousness" was first coined in 1901 by Richard Maurice Bucke. It was later popularized through the teachings of Deepak Chopra. The term is generally used to describe the concept of a universal and shared state of consciousness that transcends the intellect or capacity of any one person.

While the reference to the term itself may have been popularized recently, the concept of a shared consciousness can be traced back to ancient mythology when the Greek god Hermes and the Egyptian god Thoth were worshiped as one. It was believed that the collective intelligence of these deities was a source of great power and inspiration to all who opened themselves to the potential of their collective consciousness.

Recent thinking in physics and astronomy regarding the existence of a parallel universe or a multiverse contributes to the foundation of thought that we are all part of something much bigger and more significant than just our own lives and needs.

But the concept of melding divine intellect from an omnipotent power with human insight and inspiration can also be found in the roots of our Christian teachings. The Latin translation of the word *inspiration* is loosely "spirit within," meaning that there is a direct link between our spirituality and our level of consciousness and intellect.

Instead of searching for the hidden clues in the universe and the physical world around us for proof of a cosmic connection, perhaps we ought to apply the teachings of our Creator, however we envision Him, and realize that each of us is beautifully and uniquely made; the things that draw us together under his hand are much greater than those things that would drive us apart.

We need neither the approval nor even the recognition of others to shine as brightly as any star does in the evening sky. Each one of us brings a unique light into the universe—the gift that is our destiny and our hope.

Point of View

It seems as if we find ourselves much too often in the slack tide of our life journey. What has already passed tugs us back with an equal force of that which draws us forward.

We struggle with the images of our journey, which have flashed by us like bubbles in the rapidly moving waters on which we ride. We stand in anticipation of all that may lie before us, and we turn our heads towards the horizon as the current builds beneath our feet.

As we straddle the pushes and pulls between what was and what is yet to be, we remind ourselves that movement is often confused with progress. But progress demands that we move forward, even if the journey forward takes us back through those waters in life that we may have navigated poorly in our past.

Each reflection of ourselves in the river of life yields a unique image. What we saw yesterday is now and forever changed. What we will see tomorrow is unknown. So the only reflection we can trust is what we see today, and the only reality that we can act upon is in the present moment.

If we choose to make every present moment as perfect as it can be, we need not worry about the reflections in the water yet to come. For the waters of truth never reflect poorly on those brave enough to live out each day in great love for life and those who share it with us.

Culpable Hearts

In her '60s song "The Last Time I Saw Richard," singer-songwriter Joni Mitchell wrote that all romantics meet the same fate someday: being cynical and boring in some dark café. She goes on to paint a dark picture of a broken heart, a victim of pretty lies, and the unrealistic expectations of love and romance.

Each year, as we draw near to the magic we associate with February 14, we can easily recall past exhilarations and disappointments as we made our way through life and love. No matter the reason, a broken heart bleeds the same. We learn; we heal; we venture forward to love again.

The darkness of a love gone wrong is a shadow that casts a pall over our lives like an unwelcome cloud. But in the dimly lit recesses of our hearts, we can begin to see more clearly the true nature of love, and we realize that we often mistake romance for it.

Perhaps out of a sense of desperation or from genetic underpinnings, we eagerly give our hearts to the sweetness of romantic interactions and hopeful daydreams. We set aside the memories of painful past experiences just long enough to enjoy the present moment and feel the warmth of a new romance coming upon us, as if the sun were emerging from behind dark clouds.

Romance is like icing on a cake. It provides an immediate rush of sweet bliss and sets our hearts on fire, our pulses racing, and our minds careening between hopeful thoughts and secret wishes.

Like the icing, there is no denying the allure of romance when we happen upon it; its call on our hearts is unmistakable. But real substance and enduring satisfaction are found beneath the icing, beneath the romance. It is found in the cake, in the underlying love upon which romance is built.

What we put into the cake batter and what we put into our hearts determines the shape and form of the final product. Neither icing nor romance alone is self-sustaining.

Our true joy and satisfaction are best served in slices, so we can savor both the sweetness of romance and the fullness of love.

It seems that our Creator has endowed us with the capacity to distinguish between the things that we all experience as human beings and those that unite us spiritually.

While romance is a function of the physical world, experiencing it can amplify the spiritual connections between us. It is in these amplifications that we, as human beings, can get a glimpse of the depths of the divine love that flows through each of us.

It is this love on which we can rely when romance and the physical world let us down!

Thorn and Seed

Looking for the seeds of greatness within oneself or another is a lot like looking for flowers in the forest; sometimes you need to make your way through a lot of weeds, old wood, thorns, and clutter before you can experience the beauty that has been hiding within.

The path that we take to find this treasure can be as different and unique as each of our dreams, whether we happen upon the prize today or at some distant moment.

Though our timing and the direction of our footsteps may be uncertain, we share a common desire to discover this beauty within ourselves.

Our journey is complete when we can finally strain beyond our sense of peace and accomplishment to discover and celebrate the reflection of this beauty in all with whom we share this journey.

The Right Spin

My lovely Irish step-dancing partner in crime reminded me one morning that it was the anniversary of my cycling "accident" while we were vacationing out on Cape Cod. I've tried to pin that pedaler's punishment on her with an unwavering lack of success ever since that unfortunate incident.

While my bones took far less time to heal than my ego, and although I have since ventured on many successful rides, I still look at my bicycle and my girlfriend with both wonder and perhaps a sense of uneasiness.

Am I overly confident regarding both romance and cycling? Maybe. I do recognize, however, that there is danger in both, as there is also an alluring pleasure that is often woven in between the dangerous threads in the fabric of these realities.

But those questions can wait for another day and another ride. For now, it's time to laugh at myself and savor the humor in the memories of that unfortunate ride and the commentary of those who have profited from a good belly laugh over my misfortune.

So here it goes; the things you hear after you crash your bike and break your collarbone and ribs while vacationing on Cape Cod:

- "Boy, I bet that hurt."
- "Okay, we're on our way, but traffic is horrible" (after dialing 911).
- "You shouldn't have taken off the training wheels."
- "There were reports of significant structural damage on Cape Cod."
- "The impact would have killed off the dinosaurs."
- "Try to be comfortable; someone will see you shortly" (in hospital, in lots of pain).
- "So how are you going to blame your significant other for this?"
- "You've been selected to receive our patient care survey; what's your email address?" (still waiting to be seen and still in pain).
- "Did the EMTs ask you if your nose looked like that before the accident?"

In the future, remember that relationships are not for the faint of heart, and always ride and love with your eyes wide open!

Synchronicity of Hearts

Fall is a time of the year when we can more fully experience with our senses the forward movement of this rock upon which we stand as it makes its way on its prescribed course through the blackness of space.

The air around us begins to chill, and the trees take on a new palette of colors before shedding their delicate collection of leaves to the hardening ground below.

Our silent walks in summer sunrises are now replaced with the crackling of leaves and the whooshing of the autumn winds through the near-naked branches above.

Memories of Kate Hepburn and a golden pond come to mind, enlivening within us visions of peaceful sunsets, the call of the loons, and the warmth of a fire burning in our hearts—symbols of an unspoken commitment between two willing souls.

It occurs to me that as the number of our trips around our parent star increases and our outward vision becomes dim, we develop a much keener ability to see within. We feel the intensity of the seasons more deeply as we recall the memories and the secret callings of our hearts.

In the glow of embers that relegates the evening shadows into faint images, our minds run through all that has gone before us—our victories and our disappointments. Our promises to ourselves and others are all examined in the waning light, each assigned to a particular tick of the clock.

We begin to understand the order of importance of things in our lives. We see each new day as a beautifully wrapped gift to be opened and shared with those around us.

We hear the laughter of our grandchildren and fixate on the sparkle in their eyes as they prepare for the surprises and wonders that life holds. We stand guard over them and pledge our love and protection.

Taking advantage of the time to reflect, we examine who we are, what we have done and accomplished, what we have left undone, and what dreams we still hold deep within the quiet recesses of our hearts.

In the silence of the season, amid the dying embers and recollections of those moments in life that have left the deepest marks upon our memories, we come to a new realization.

While we may set aside a special day now and then to remember the connections in our lives that are closest to our hearts, we need to remind ourselves that love, like fine wine, is best enjoyed when shared with many.

Love commands us to explore the possibilities and character in all our connections as God's children. Our task is to peer through the cloudy moments of uncertainty and find the light of love in the hearts of our brothers and sisters, to fully appreciate the diversity of creation, and to help each other discover our Creator's plan of good for each of us.

As we do this, we not only multiply the flow of love from within ourselves, but we create a torrent of goodwill, joy, and respect that has the power to wash away the doubts, negativity, and fear in the waters around us. Only then is each of us and our world transformed by the stillness and joy found in peaceful, loving hearts.

We begin to understand that our appreciation for Kate Hepburn, a golden pond, a crackling fire, and the change of season is but a reflection of our desire to find a steadfast love and the security of a weathered but enduring partnership.

We understand, too, that what matters most is not in which cycle of our years we find that one enduring partnership, but that we recognize it when it comes into our lives and cherish each tick of the clock and each step of our journey forward…together!

In the Storm

Amid the storm, we often fail to realize that the waves tossing us about at the height of peril are of similar form and substance as those upon which we glide to safe harbor. We are merely being tested to see how well we navigate our way through them.

Our reactions to the world around us don't define the realities of the space in which we breathe. They instead determine our makeup and our ability to look beyond ourselves and beyond the confusion and chaos of the present to the true nature of our being and the spirit that lives within.

We all go through periods in life when the storms of change, loss, disappointment, or heartbreak seem to pour upon us in unceasing and cruel regularity. We come to expect the worst, so those expectations often become more easily realized. In these times of darkness, we are challenged to find the light in our souls and in the memories of past sunrises.

While Scripture reminds us that rain falls on both the just and the unjust, we are left searching for a way out of the storm to calmer times and more peaceful waters. What we often fail to recognize is that the way out of the storm is not to stop focusing on the things happening around us, but instead to focus on how we respond to those things.

In our moments of gloom and uncertainty, we need to remind ourselves that the light of the peaceful dawn, which we seek, shines from within us. Though it may be temporarily hidden by the clouds that creep into our hearts, it shines with a reassuring glow and a warmth that promises to light our way forward in the darkness and to burn away the clouds of life's challenges. A gift from our Creator, it is there for us to find and to brighten our days if we have faith and the courage to look for it.

Spanish String Theory

To be students of life, it's necessary to immerse ourselves in the physical world that surrounds us.

We dive into a sensory buffet of sun, sky, sea, sand, or the panoramic opulence found on a distant mountaintop as we gaze into the distance and contemplate our insignificance and how lucky we are to have experienced that exact moment.

It seems that at times, fate reveals its unspoken promises to us in ways that allow us to more fully comprehend the grandeur and magnitude of the world around us.

Perhaps the same is true of our emotional mountaintops. We struggle at times with the ups and downs of our daily lives, wondering what the connection is between us and others.

We seek certainties and absolutes. We climb the mountain of emotional awareness and are surprised and disappointed when the vision that unfolds before us is not what we expected.

We lose sight of the significance of each step taken as we ascend that mountain. We forget the images that our eyes and minds captured as we made our journey upward, of the victories we experienced one inch, one step at a time.

Then perhaps, one day, maybe in the softness of a summer breeze, as our life is winding down, we hear the gentle fingering of a Spanish guitar. Each note reaches deep into our hearts and connects a forgotten victory to a counterpoint in our souls, and we smile, reassured that our journey was not without purpose, nor was it without a plan for our good.

A Cut Above

Between the Rainbows

It was a time of great personal upheaval. I found myself wedged between a world of Western casual travel and Middle Eastern simplicities as I winged my way through the night sky, bouncing off clouds under the light of a full moon.

The smell of curry was thick in the air as my neighbors, both fore and aft, left and right, were dark-skinned with raven hair and mysteriously dressed, as if a Halloween party had never ended, or perhaps they were recreating a vintage episode from *The Twilight Zone*.

Nonetheless, I made my way over the cold waters of the North Atlantic, where soon the gales of November would whip the waters beneath me into a frenzied frappé of winter misery–so much better to be traveling above all of that meteorological discord.

The rough weather below seemed to pale in comparison to the storms I had been experiencing for most of my last five trips around our home star. Broken promises, shattered dreams, and instability had me waking up in the morning and detesting the image staring back at me as I quickly sought to remove the unwanted debris from my face. If I could only remove the other undesirable things in my life as easily!

But the whiskers proved more willing to be removed than the troubles and heartache with which I had gone to bed for the past five years. Perhaps the business trip I was about to embark on would magically bring everything into focus and quiet my mind.

So I had squeezed myself into the tiniest piece of upholstered real estate; at least I had one arm free to the aisle. Listening to a collection of Bach sonatas as I typed out a few thoughts about a recent interlude with an interesting woman, an unleashed spirit who fears that she is awkward and directionally challenged, but thoroughly enjoyable.

I began to get lost in my memories, in the words I had put into life, and I started thinking about possibilities and what it means to be an authentic person. I thought about how much I missed being in a loving relationship with a special person, even if just for a moment. I thought about how wonderful it would feel to be a part of something special with an equally special someone.

I closed my eyes and dreamed how wonderful the feeling would be to fall asleep each night after kissing the woman I loved and how comforting it would be to roll over on my side, put my arm around a woman who loved me in equal measure, and let her know that I will stand beside her in life, just as I lie beside her in bed.

I imagined with a sigh just what it might feel like to pull her into me and brush her warmth against my body, how special it would be to express our love for each other in a dance of passion and personal surrender that would draw us into each other physically, emotionally, and spiritually until we melted into one form and one consciousness.

I stopped typing for a moment, gathered myself, and remembered that personal integrity is an essential part of the equation, the formula for both balance and peace in our lives; it is an integral part of a loving relationship. Integrity drives us to consider our responsibilities, commitments, and choices in all aspects of our lives.

If we strive to become a person of high integrity, we can't help but become a more authentic person. In this process, we open ourselves to the fullness of life and the peace that comes with being authentic to our spiritual nature.

This got me thinking about the special people in my life and how important it was to pause and reflect and be thankful for the friends I have and how true friendship is unbounded by distance or time, and how the embodiment of authenticity is simply truth in action, benevolence, and sincerity in all that we do.

Those reflections brought me back to thinking about a long-legged Irish lass fate had determined would find her clippers in my thinning locks and who would eventually Irish step dance her way into my heart.

Years later, my hairline is higher, my temples are a bit greyer, but my heart is so much fuller. The ups and downs of daily living, along with all the challenges that seemed to be a part of each day on this spinning stone, now seem more manageable and of diminished importance.

The face staring back at me in the mirror now wears a broad smile and radiates a quiet confidence in the knowledge that true love heals the most damaged of hearts. The plan of good, which our Creator reveals to each of us one heartbeat at a time, has already found its place in my life. It abides joyfully and willingly in a heart now eager to take the next few steps in life's never-ending dance!

Measure Up

As the aforementioned greying of my temples reflects the distance that I've traveled on my life journey, I wish that there was a similar measure that would allow me to see more clearly the many blessings that have been poured out upon me as I make my way up and around the curves of my path to destiny.

Of course, the obvious blessings are not forgotten. Health, prosperity, friends and family, the laughter of my children and my grandchildren—these are readily available for my enjoyment and my reassurance that I have indeed been blessed.

However, the part of my existential maturation that enables me to connect my life experiences with those blessings is not yet fully capable of revealing the accurate measure of my good fortune.

It seems to me that some spiritual barometer would help connect all of the disparate activities and occurrences in my dance with destiny, the result of which would be a much better understanding of the width and breadth of all of life's blessings that I've experienced, both seen and unseen.

Perhaps if we had some way of measuring our level of empathy, we could prepare ourselves better for enjoying the blessings already received in our lives and those still to come.

Empathy seems to sharpen our sensitivity to the world around us and to the people with whom we interact. It opens our eyes and our minds to comparisons of all types.

Once we have an expanded awareness of the people around us, we are then more ready to connect what we see and observe in others with our own experiences in life.

Empathy allows us to make comparisons with others that are both quantitative and qualitative. That, in turn, becomes a basis for examining our own lives and the measure of blessings we have experienced. Once we have achieved that awareness, we are then ready to move forward to the next step in developing a complete picture of the fullness of our blessings by developing our spiritual empathy.

To fully appreciate the blessings in our lives, we must come to realize that all blessings, whether in our own lives or those of others, are interconnected. More than just realizing that all blessings come from the same omnipotent source, we need to understand that the blessings poured out onto others impact and amplify the blessings that we have already received and those still to come.

We are all connected. We are all cut from the same spiritual cloth. The true blessings of life are not exclusive to us; they are available to all who open themselves to discovering the seeds of greatness already planted within each of us and in others.

Unhurried Blessings

I've heard it said, "Never trust a person who uses thirty words to say what could have been said in eight!"

While each of us has undoubtedly struggled at times to rein in either our verbose declarations or those of someone around us, there is a more unsettling undertone to this ripple of impatience.

One of the benefits and the challenges from the evolution of technology over the past several decades has been the push to do things more quickly. Aside from faster computers, bullet trains, space travel, and the internet, the "do it now" mantra and the desire for immediate results and instant gratification have infiltrated all aspects of our thinking.

Too often, our path in life is altered because we long to see what is coming or wish to hasten reaching the next hilltop in our journey. We become so fixated on the need to move forward and see what lies on the other side of the next hill that we barely have time to appreciate the blessings that surround us where we stand today.

While our Creator has placed seeds of greatness within each of us, those seeds grow at the right time. The blessings we receive in life help to nurture the growth of those seeds.

Each day must be lived one second at a time so that we can absorb each drop of rain, each ray of sunshine, and each moment of beauty. Similarly, it is with the blessings we receive in our lives that we can more fully appreciate them over time through the lens of insight and the growth of our wisdom.

Empty Glass

I came across a sculpture entitled *Emptiness*. It was captured as a digital photo by a friend of mine in India. The piece was created by an artist who had lost a child. The creator intended to convey the feeling of emptiness and total loss in dealing with life's most difficult challenges. The piece is compelling and does a fantastic job of describing the indescribable.

While I have only experienced this type of loss from an arm's length, I have come to understand that no words can describe the feelings of a parent who has lost a child long before their expected time on this twisted stone has ended. There is no good way to spin the story, and the glass is neither half full nor half empty; it is instead devoid of all content.

When we face one of life's many difficulties and seek counsel from our friends or family, we are often encouraged to remain positive, even in the presence of worry, disappointment, or discord.

We often hear the suggestion "Look at the glass as half-filled." While we may understand the intent of this suggestion, it rarely helps us to resolve whatever issue in life we are facing at that moment, and it only goes a short way in providing comfort and reassurance when dealing with the biggest challenges in life.

While we do not know the length of our days in this oftentimes cruel world, we do know that we shall live out our days as our Creator has appointed for each of us. Whether young or old, we are called to the same ultimate destiny.

We can only celebrate the present and make the most of our journey through life in harmony with one another. For as we share a common grief and emptiness in the face of life's most significant challenges, we also have the ability and a mandate to share love, compassion, and a spirit that connects each of us to those who have already made their way home.

In the Shadow of Our Conscience

Each year, as we approach the end of yet another orbit around our parent star, we may find ourselves reflecting on the future and the ultimate gift of love that was bestowed upon us so long ago. It is a poignant reminder that the future is promised to no one. While the number of our days remains unknown, we have the opportunity to live each day as if it were our last and to ask ourselves some critical questions.

Would we seek forgiveness for the times we have hurt or disappointed others? Would we offer our forgiveness freely and without conditions? Would we find it within ourselves to forgive our own mistakes and shortcomings? Would we express our love more often, asking others, "How can I help"? Would we acknowledge our achievements, no matter how small or insignificant they may seem, and say to ourselves, "I'm proud of who I am and what I have accomplished!"?

Would we replace sarcasm and impatience with kindness and understanding in our interactions with family, friends, and strangers? Would we listen more and speak less? Would we celebrate the holiday season for the miracle of promises fulfilled and the hope for a better world? Would we have the courage to live out our faith in our daily lives?

As the Greek philosopher Socrates wisely stated many hundreds of years ago, "The unexamined life is not worth living." This timeless wisdom encourages us to reflect deeply on our actions, our relationships, and our purpose, and to strive for a life of meaning and fulfillment.

A Concinnated Calling

The grey November skies have stubbornly given themselves over to December's frosty dawns and chilling winds. The first blanketing of winter white is already rolled out upon the countryside, silencing the landscape and preparing us for the bitterness that will surely follow.

Our steps quicken in response to the falling temperatures, and we feel the wetness of our breath upon our face as we scurry around the neighborhood looking for the next item on our list of Christmas treasures.

We approach our tasks with laser focus, stopping occasionally for a latte to keep our heartbeats aligned with the importance of our work. Tradition demands that we finish our tasks on time. Weeks of hunting, hours of wrapping, minutes of opening—most will be forgotten in seconds.

Somewhere beneath the shredded wrapping paper amid the emptied boxes and the hollow echoes of surprises realized or forgotten, there is a presence, a consciousness, that has stumbled into the maze of ribbons and glitter, waiting to be discovered.

It is something very subtle and personal, yet it speaks to each of us, resonating in our minds and hearts with a nagging demand for our attention. We try to quiet our minds and reflect on the smiles and the looks of surprise on the faces of all those with whom we shared our treasures, but to no avail.

We sense a vacuum, or perhaps some indignation, realizing that something has been forgotten, lost among the torn wrapping paper, strewn ribbons, and faded smiles.

We close our eyes and take a deep breath. We travel back in our memory to a time when our excitement peaked with the setting up of the Nativity scene and placing the worn statue of that tiny cherub into its manger.

We are reminded of the gifts we received from family and friends, and we smile. We are reminded, too, of the gift that was born unto all of us so long ago, a spirit within each of us, waiting for our full acceptance and celebration. Accepting the invitation, we are now complete!

A Christmas Wish

One of my favorite meditations goes something like this: "Look to this day, for yesterday is but a dream and tomorrow only a vision, but today well-lived makes every yesterday a dream of happiness and every tomorrow a vision of hope!" I don't know the author, but I do know that whoever wrote those words had figured out one of life's greatest truisms and goals.

Like threads in the blanket of creation, we are all pulled in many directions. What happens at one end of the blanket affects our immediate patch of threads. However slightly we may be pulled one way or the other, our life's path changes constantly.

Change may come as a whisper in the wheatfields of our lives, or it may arrive in the form of a tempest, but we can count on the certainty of change and on the demands that change makes of us to adapt and to keep moving forward on our life path.

When I first hung my children's handmade ornaments on our Christmas tree, I thought that I knew what life was about and where the journey would take me. Not surprisingly, the twists and turns of my life that would follow repeatedly demonstrated how little I knew about life and how unprepared I was to accept change during those times. How do we prepare ourselves for the unknown?

It has been my experience, acquired through a variety of changes and course corrections throughout my life, that there is no way to prepare ourselves for that which we cannot reasonably predict as we move forward on our life's journey.

Yes, we can save for our retirement, eat properly, and exercise, but we can't plan for the truly unknown. So, then, how do we move forward, down our current path in life without fear of the unknown, without fear of change?

There is a part of Buddhism that teaches us to view life experiences and changes in life as if they were our friends. It suggests that we welcome them into our lives and see them as part of our destiny, not as changes to it. We remain in control of our lives, but we learn how to incorporate changes in our daily lives.

I don't know that I entirely agree with this view of life, but I have come to understand that accepting change is far healthier and ultimately more rewarding than denying or rejecting it.

Perhaps the way to strike a balance between the uncertainty of life and the acceptance of life's changes is to take a more granular look at our current path in life. Focusing on each day, one day at a time, helps us both manage the anxiety of reacting to things that may never happen and deal with those that do.

Perhaps if we fill our day celebrating who we are, reviewing what we have learned on our journey, and welcoming tomorrow as part of God's plan for our lives, we will indeed dream of happiness and look on tomorrow as a vision of hope.

Breakfast in a Parallel Universe

P oet Maya Angelou once wrote, "Life is not about the breaths you take, but about the moments that take your breath away."

That to me is the essence of finding passion in life's wrinkles as we surf the wormholes of our universe, looking for a deeper meaning to our existence and seeking to connect the pieces of our daily living into a strand of shiny memories, like pearls, that will adorn our lives and endure the scrutiny of our reflection and self-assessment.

Each new dawn brings with it an opportunity to discover yet another tiny globe to sew on our string. We breach the silence of the new day by giving thanks and praise to our Creator. Then we become slaves to the daily routines that find their way into our lives with both subtle and profound impacts; they become one with the fabric of our lives and in many ways help to define us, or at the very least, they help to paint a picture of how we wish to be perceived by others.

With that in mind, I found myself jumping from cloud to cloud as I made my way from Connecticut to Abu Dhabi, then to India, back to Connecticut, to Costa Rica, to Mexico, and finally back home to Connecticut once again. During the distant travels, I found myself giving thanks and sharing some of those experiences with new friends and their families, as well as with those closest to my heart.

I can scarcely believe how blessed and humbled I am to be doing what I am doing, meeting so many wonderful people and seeing such beauty and diversity in life. That beauty may reside in the face of a beautiful woman, in the shadows of a mountain valley, in a tropical sunrise, or in the bright eyes of hope and possibility of our children.

While our Creator's plan for each of us may include unequal amounts of opportunity and challenge, it is by our hand and our hard work, by our faith, and by our living in humility and thanksgiving that we magnify our blessings in whatever form and quantity they may be, and in so doing, we squeeze the most joy out of our lives.

As we experience these periods of reflection and digestion, we examine ourselves and the patchwork of our daily activities, trying to determine what to keep and what to discard. We reshuffle the color, content, and overall design to form a more updated and relevant picture of ourselves and how we want to structure our day, as well as what we want to accomplish in this tiniest slice of our lives.

For me, most of my years on this twisted stone have included a portion of my day allotted to breakfast at a local eatery of one kind or another. Perhaps it is an overwhelming need for socialization, or maybe a latent need for validation, or the opportunity to have an audience with whom I can interact. Whatever the reason, stirring the clouds of milk in my coffee, accompanied by a familiar crowd, has become an essential part of my life.

I'm sure that there are well-established pathways of neurons deep within my brain that allow me to stumble my way unconsciously to my favorite breakfast spot in zombielike fashion, the same way an oscillating sprinkler cycles through its duties in watering the lawn with a never-ending repetition of practiced and precise movements.

So I found myself stuck in a pattern of morning behavior that seemed more ritual than routine, the calling more than a hunger for breakfast fare. Acknowledging that, I pointed my vehicle once again down the road towards Main Street, where my hunger could be satisfied both literally and on some other unknown level.

The traffic was predictable as I turned the corner off North Main Street and headed south across the railroad tracks, past the old North End Firehouse, towards the center of town and closer to the source of this unexplained call. No surprises: a school bus here, a delivery truck there, a jogger making his way up the street where so many had passed by in crazy costumes and headwear just a few days earlier for the annual Thanksgiving Day Road Race. All seemed as it should be.

Acknowledging the traffic light at the top of Main Street, I headed downhill. Just in front of the large window overlooking Main Street, I coasted into my usual parking spot, which provided a warning to those who huddled inside the café of who would be next to satisfy their hunger and curiosity over breakfast while communing with the regulars. Grabbing my keys and my iPad, I stepped out onto the street, locked the doors with a confirming chirp from my vehicle, and headed down the sidewalk towards the restaurant.

It was a cold morning. My breath poured out of my mouth like an old steam engine as, just before the entrance to the café, I walked past two souls huddled in the small alcove where they took pleasure from the few remaining puffs of their cigarettes. I nodded a good morning to them and walked the remaining few steps to the door of the restaurant.

As I opened the door to step inside, I could hear the church bell on the hill across the street from me clanging three times, as if it were heralding my arrival, or maybe issuing a warning to me or those inside the restaurant. No matter what, my routine would not be denied. I pressed forward through the entrance into the warmth of my breakfast enclave.

As my eyes struggled to adjust to the dimmer interior lights, the well-traveled pathways deep in my brain easily compensated for the temporary lack of vision and guided me faithfully to my regular seat at the corner of the breakfast bar, a much-coveted piece of real estate. I shed my jacket and climbed onto the barstool, adjusting its position to the precise distance required between stool and counter.

I had barely settled in when a tall mug of steaming black addiction was placed in front of me, accompanied by a small pitcher of cream and a tired greeting from one of the servers. The look on his face could have easily been replaced with a sign on his forehead saying, "As if my day hasn't been tough enough already, now I have to deal with you!"

"And a good morning to you, sir," I blurted out as he disappeared into the kitchen area without acknowledging me or my weak attempt at conversation.

Experience in this establishment had taught me that conversation and interaction were best saved for a time after things had been resettled, just as you wait for the ripples in a pool to subside before getting a clear look at what is hiding beneath the surface of the water. I pulled the steaming mug closer to me, picked up my spoon, reached for the small container, and completed the familiar combination of coffee, sweetener, and cream.

Mixing the brown liquid with the right amount of cream and swirling the concoction with my spoon, I waited for the mixture to cool. I investigated the cup and tried to find any remaining clouds, wanting to complete the job, but it was done; the formulary was complete, one uniform color and the same consistency throughout. Now, it had cooled enough to enjoy.

As I began to sip the reassuring brew, I became more aware of my surroundings as I listened and observed the conversations and events happening around me. To my left, a pretty redheaded woman in conversation with the same server who had delivered my coffee and then disappeared a few minutes earlier; to my right, a shaggy-haired man three days past needing a shave, clutching a pearl-handled cane and sorely in need of some positive thinking as he muttered something about his disdain for the cold and his aggravation with his former spouse, leaving me confused about which complaint was real and which was just part of a mantra of daily annoyances that needed to be aired.

One by one, the regulars filed in, each taking their place at the breakfast counter and receiving a similar greeting and response from our server, while acknowledging each other with a familiar mixture of politeness and indifference.

The ritual continued for us all as we each issued our instructions and orders, ensuring that our breakfasts would arrive precisely as we desired. In turn, we received a similar and predictable response from our grumpy server, who once again had found his way to the casino the previous night, returning home with little cash and even less patience for us in the morning that followed.

It was all so familiar—a blend of reassurance, ritual, and repartee that bound our days together like threads in a quilt, different threads going in different directions, yet all one with the fabric of our daily lives. There was no need to analyze any further. Whatever the direction our lives took from that time forward, our day and our lives would be woven together for good or bad as the fabric of our existence was stitched into place.

At the day's end, we will conjure up bits and pieces from our breakfast conversations that morning, and we will find some form of entertainment value, perhaps even some insight that had eluded our thinking until we brought it to the breakfast counter that day.

At night, we will lie in our beds and reflect on the words, the faces, and the impressions from our breakfast encounter. We will stir the memories in our minds, just as we do our morning coffee, until the memories all disappear into one blur of cloudy sameness.

With our eyes growing heavy and just before giving in to the night, we will remind ourselves that, no matter where we are, we pick up our spoon and drop it into the amber goodness of our morning ritual. The swirling clouds within our cup all melt into a oneness of color and consistency.

We will close our eyes and surrender to sleep with a smile on our faces, realizing that the key ingredients for living our lives in happiness and authenticity, however we may choose to define them, can be found in between the ripples within our coffee cup.

As it is with those ripples, though ours is a singular journey, how we interact with each other, especially those with whom we share our daily routines, affects everyone with whom we come in contact. Forever forward, we are changed; forever forward, we are as one.

Cold Calculations

Winter is upon us; the mornings are dark, and the sun hides behind a frozen sky as if to deny us the light and warmth we seek.

We struggle to leave the comfort of our beds and move our bodies forward on our journey. But the demands of our day call us, and we reluctantly relent. We pour ourselves out into the cold reality of today, and we take a few cautious steps into our practiced routines and our destiny.

We reach for our morning coffee with half-opened eyes and a quiet denial of our awakening. We stir the clouds in our coffee cup as we begin to anticipate what the day may hold. We look through the window to the darkness of the world outside; the grey skies confirm the coming dawn, yet we still struggle to embrace what awaits us in the day ahead.

As we begin to awaken fully to the new day, we may be interrupted by a flash of yesterday—a disappointment, an angry word, a moment of betrayal perhaps—whatever the source, the unpleasant memories blow through our minds like unwanted seeds trying to take root in our hearts and sprout new shafts of bitterness, growing obstacles on our path forward.

We pause a moment and remind ourselves that yesterday is now just a dream. Tomorrow is only a vision. But today is our opportunity to create a new vision and memory for tomorrow. Compassion is the key that frees a heart frozen in bitterness and allows the healing powers of forgiveness to soothe the soul.

Sweet Arrival

Mitch's Way

It was fate that had you fall into our lives, in the midst of a crowd of siblings eager to share a smile and pull at your curly locks; it was a welcome, a sign of our acceptance and enduring love.

We each grew up knowing our secret thoughts and sharing only the ones we all could laugh at and feel resonate within our bones. Our secret places remained our mystery, and the tree outside our window became full of our thoughts, words, and laughter, each leaf a dream belonging to one of us, belonging to all of us.

Somehow, we found our paths in life, the width and breadth befitting the destinies awaiting each of us. While we walked together for only a short time, the echoes of laughter we left in that special tree continue to fill our minds and warm our hearts with every autumn breeze and each moonlit summer night.

Life required that most of us tend to our responsibilities and the task of acquiring those things that can be counted and categorized. It consumed many of us for far too long and many times broke our spirits. But we endured; we overcame the obstacles and our insecurities.

But you had different ideas of what life was supposed to be. You counted full moons and shooting stars while we wrote checks and paid taxes. We took pictures of our vacations and then struggled to return to the realities of working life. You made a life out of vacation pictures and struggled to return to the best places to watch for shooting stars and follow the endless procession of waves arriving onshore under a silvery moon.

Now, as our paths in life begin to converge, we see, with widened eyes and minds and hearts awakened, the possibility that we have traveled on the exact path that fate predestined for each of us. We come now to a place where we can more easily accept the realization that there is no right path or wrong path; there is only *our* path.

So we say goodbye for now to one of our kind—someone who was made of similar substance and form, someone who dreamed and laughed as we did, someone who left echoes of that laughter in the tree outside our window, and someone who, as all of us eventually shall do, has found his time and his way home!

Wonder of Night

My amazement is unending each time that I gaze up at a clear night sky and allow myself to take in the fullness of the heavens sparkling above me.

It is a palette awash with twinkling specks across the blackness, with wisps of milky starlight whipped into a broad stroke that stretches our imagination as much as it does our visual acuity.

My head is filled with numbers: two trillion galaxies, two hundred billion stars in each, and countless planets whirling through space. The sheer number of objects in the universe is well beyond our collective abilities to comprehend. So we draw in a deep breath, shake our heads in wonder, and ponder the huge questions of our existence.

We are fearful, in part, that we are not alone in this universe. The reality may be that we are not as special and unique a specimen of creation as we perhaps once thought.

The inverse is equally unsettling to us—in the mind-numbing vastness of creation, all we have to illuminate the blackness surrounding this twisting blue stone we share is each other and the starlight that falls upon us.

Perhaps, then, it would be more beneficial for us to turn our attention away from the shadowy expanse above our heads, focusing instead on the threads of reality and oneness of creation into which we have been carefully woven.

In so doing, maybe we will discover and learn to appreciate that we are individual grains of sand on the beach of humankind, drawing strength and courage from our common beginnings, and wonder and expectation from our shared destiny.

Maybe then we will come to the common realization that what lies in the depths of space isn't nearly as important as what lies within our hearts.

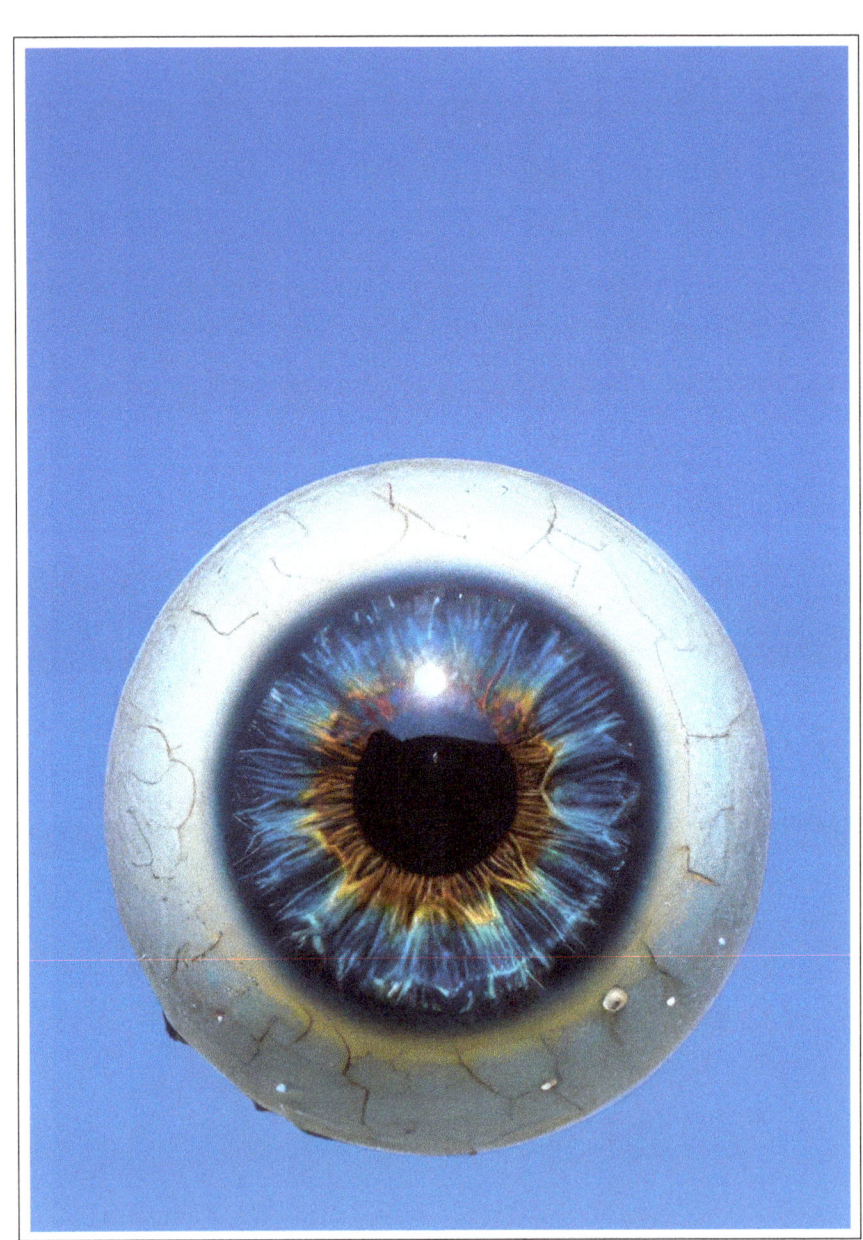

Eye of the Beholder

One of the most remarkable aspects of being human is our capacity to find beauty in various forms. It's almost as if we are programmed to discover beauty and value in our lives and the world around us.

Beyond the natural world, we can also find beauty in other areas of our lives. We see it in a painting, a sculpture, a song, a dance, and a written word. We can even find it in a particularly pleasing piece of architecture that strikes a chord within us and reverberates in our minds, hearts, and souls. Indeed, it seems as if we are programmed to discover the beauty around us.

Every day, we are presented with numerous opportunities to find beauty in our lives. For the most part, we are willing to take advantage of this opportunity. We either appreciate that moment as we experience it, or we hold it in our memory, attempting to recall it and savor the moment in greater fullness during quiet moments of reflection.

The desire to find beauty around us and within our lives appears to be a part of our innate nature. I experienced this myself just recently during a particularly nasty spring storm.

The warmth of the season was on my doorstep. The newly planted shrubs were beginning to come alive again. The tulips and hyacinths were already peeking through their covers and welcoming the warming sun. The grass was starting to green, and the trees were showing their first signs of budding. While the view from my doorstep was appealing, I found myself anxious for the fullness of the spring season still several weeks away.

A few days later, a particularly nasty spring storm rolled through my neighborhood. It brought with it a deluge of heavy rain and wind, gusting at times to nearly hurricane force. My windows rattled as the heavy rain and wind assaulted my house and everything in my garden. Once the rain subsided and the wind gusts became less frequent, I cautiously opened my front door to get a better view of my yard and to survey what damage may have been done by the storm.

I poked my head out the door, still needing to dodge the occasional gust of wind. As I surveyed the front yard, I could quickly concede that no real damage had occurred; my trees were all intact, gutters attached, and siding still in place. As I brought my focus down to my newly planted landscaping and the flowers that had been waiting for the spring sun, to my surprise, hidden among the emerging tulips and other assorted perennials was an outcropping of tiny purple flowers surrounded by a spread of delicate green shafts and dark-green leaves. It was, by far, the most beautiful specimen in my garden, and it was so unexpected. A surprise perhaps? Something planted by the previous owners for their enjoyment and now bursting forward after the warm spring rains? More beauty in my life had arrived.

Moments like these need to be captured and shared with others who can appreciate both the beauty of the discovery and the surprise of the moment. So I grabbed my phone and again leaned out my front door to snap a picture. I quickly viewed and edited the photo, and then proudly sent it off to a friend who I was certain would find great delight in the unexpected beauty now revealed in my garden.

A few minutes later, I received a text message from her with a brief comment and a question: *Really beautiful. Have you checked your front door? Is your wreath still there?*

Yep, she was right once again.

As I said, we are programmed to find beauty wherever we can. Beauty knows no age or social status; it has no memory of past failures or unrealized dreams. It obeys no boundaries for sharing or limits to a loving heart.

Beauty finds no comfort in the pain of another nor recoils in condescending pretense to the cries of the poor and oppressed. Beauty finds its reflection in the longing hearts of others and seeks residence in the quiet corners of a contemplative mind.

Beauty is the personification of all these things in a fabric of many threads, a patchwork of many colors, textures, and visions that walks alongside us.

Beauty is the realization that you make a difference in this life one heart, one mind at a time if you dare to let it be so! Let's commit ourselves to finding it in each other. That is the real beauty!

Mindful Dissonance

In psychology, the term "cognitive dissonance" refers to a situation in which a person holds two or more contradictory beliefs, ideas, or values, or participates in an action that contradicts one of these elements, both of which cause internal stress and anxiety. An example would be a person choosing to smoke even though they know that smoking causes cancer. That conflict in values or beliefs produces unsettling discord within that person.

Mindfulness is the psychological process of purposely, without judgment, paying attention to experiences occurring in the present moment. Life sometimes assaults us with both forced mindfulness and the dissonance produced when we are suddenly confronted with the realities of the present.

In the era of COVID-19, we were challenged to put some of our values, ideas, or beliefs on hold. We were asked to modify our behaviors in ways that were not easy. In many cases, these behaviors extended far beyond our past experiences or our comfort levels. We were thrust into an unfamiliar routine that not only forced us to distance ourselves from one another, but also to isolate ourselves from families, friends, and familiar sources of comfort and support. We were confronted by a situation that demanded we focus on the present.

While the waters of discord rush at us with increasing pace and volume, we must still navigate our way down this river we share. We are all rocked by the same turbulence; we all strain to catch glimpses of what lies ahead for us. We all have too many questions and too few answers.

Although we may all be victims of forced mindfulness and the discomfort of conflicting values, we still can surround ourselves with a spiritual buffer that allows us to navigate our way through these troubled waters without completely losing our sense of who we are by reminding ourselves we were made in His image.

Within each of us have been sown the seeds of greatness that will drive our movement forward on our life journey, and He has provided us with the comfort and awareness that we are all singular and unique threads in a patchwork of humanity. We are all interconnected. We are never alone. We must remind ourselves that not only do we share a common challenge, but we also dip our cups into the same spiritual well. How much we drink is ours to decide!

Reflecting Pool

In the book of Proverbs, it is written that "just as water reflects the face, so one human heart reflects another." Mahatma Gandhi shared, "The best way to find yourself is to lose yourself in the service of others." Though we travel on paths that twist and turn in unique response to each of our footsteps, our destination is a shared vision of fullness of heart and peaceful exuberance.

We pass each other along the journey at many crossroads. Each encounter provides an opportunity to interact with one another, to bring sunshine into another's heart, to lighten another's load, and to fill their minds with the peace of love and oneness of purpose. In doing so, we fill ourselves with the riches of a giving heart. We warm ourselves in the glow of brotherhood.

Our steps lighten as we make our way towards our shared destiny. While the waters of life flow by us with ever-increasing speed, occasionally we happen upon pools of quiet where we can catch a glimpse of ourselves in the stillness.

Our greatest joy on this journey comes from finding a reflection that smiles back with a whole heart and the confidence of knowing that we have made a positive difference in the lives of those with whom we share our journey.

Progressive Assurance

It seems at times that we find ourselves caught between the road to hell and the stairway to heaven.

Whether we plan our steps with great care or throw caution to the wind and charge forward, we inevitably end up, at some point on our journey, wondering if we are on the right path and if our destination is what we had hoped.

It may be our genetic makeup and evolutionary roots that are responsible for the confusion, caution, and drive we exhibit on our journey through life, but, whatever the reason, our journey forward is not an option; it has been predetermined.

Life demands that we move forward even when we can't always see what lies ahead for us. We can, however, decide how we will respond to all that we encounter in the waiting sunlight and in the shadows.

Any challenge that we may face—as we ride this twisting stone along with those whom we love and with whom we share our destiny—can be viewed as just one step and point in time, not as our final destination or the purpose for our existence.

Where we stand today on our journey is the result of each step that we have chosen to take along the way. We can't go back in time and redo our steps; we can, however, change direction and use our intellect, insights, and spiritual inspiration to more carefully consider each step forward, upward, or otherwise.

We can also remember that our Creator made our faces for smiling. While our road in life is often rough and uncertain, an unrelenting smile always seems to smooth our steps and lighten our load!

Arrogant Ambivalence

A friend of mine once told me that she looks at life as a present—something beautifully boxed and wrapped, found at the foot of her bed every morning. Each day, she wakes up with excitement and the anticipation of unwrapping this gift and discovering something new, exciting, or fulfilling.

No doubt, the reality of our daily challenges and the news we take in throughout each day threatens our exuberance for life, yet we are compelled to unwrap this gift and discover what life holds for us. While we may unwrap a day filled with challenges and uncomfortable amounts of discord, the alternative is to ignore the opportunity for great joy in discovering the hidden beauty in life's wrinkles.

While, each day, we may find kindred spirits who share the same excitement for living as we do, we are inevitably confronted by cynics and those who seem obsessed with pointing out the shortcomings of our gifts and the opportunities of each day. We know their names; we know their familiar songs of lamentation and their arrogance about their disappointment with their lot in life. They not only refuse to see beauty and possibility in each day of their existence, but they also distort our vision of the possibilities and experiences of our day.

Perhaps their reluctance to accept the possibility of discovering a day with opportunities for joy and a positive outcome is a result of some deeply held conviction about their worthiness, as if they feel undeserving of finding joy each day. They seem unwilling to accept the possibility of anything good happening in their lives. For these people, the glass is always half empty; the rain only falls on them.

Though we may try to help them look at themselves and their lives in different ways, we need to insulate ourselves from the flow of negativity that seems to pour out of them. The irony of these people is that while they are desperate to experience joy and the possibilities of the positive, they increasingly distance themselves from those possibilities by their actions.

As people of faith, we are challenged to provide comfort and inclusion to all people. It may be difficult—in fact, near impossible at times—but we need to call to mind the mandate of the One who left us here; He commanded us to love one another. In our efforts to be accepting of those who rain on our parade, we have the best chance to bring sunshine into their lives and further extend the joy and surprise of the gift we have already opened!

Paternal Exuberance

Though the gate through which the great surprises and unexpected realities of my life become more distant, enough time remains for welcomed insights into the decades of learning and life that have already passed by.

Life and death, friends and strangers, victories and regrets have all flourished in the fields where I have planted my seeds as I grew alongside my hopes and dreams of life, love, and mindfulness in my journey towards destiny.

Life has provided many surprises for me; some are good, some debilitating, and others are still waiting to be fully understood. On balance, though, my glass has always been more filled than not, and my view of life and my place in it has been one of joy.

One of the things for which I am most grateful is the profound opportunity I have been given to be a father and to see my sons become the individuals they are. Each is so different; each has traveled a different path in life, yet each abides by a covenant made with his Creator to nurture the seeds of greatness planted within.

Though the complications in my journey prevented me from sharing some of the twists and turns of their progress towards destiny, enough have made it into the recesses of my mind and heart to sustain me and fuel my hopes of having been the father that I needed to be.

While life has taught me much about who I am and what I aspire to be, my children have helped shape me into my unique form of personhood—part friend, part teacher, part student, and eternal comforter. They have smoothed out the sharpest edges of my persona and helped me to take an extra breath between each step in life.

Most importantly, they have opened my mind and heart to experiencing unconditional love, and they have demonstrated the same capacity and joy in their relationships with their children and those closest to their hearts. What else can a father wish for himself and his children?

Bright Idea

Life always teaches us things along our journey if we remain open to receiving these insights and learnings. However, we also learn at an early age that some of those lessons are painful.

Whether it is a disappointment suffered by us as a child, an unmet expectation in our adult life, or a feeling of loss as we look back on our lives, we often respond to these unpleasant feelings by putting a shell around ourselves to protect our healing hearts. While this response to the unpleasant learnings in life is entirely understandable, responding in this way creates more difficulties for us.

The trouble is that when we isolate our emotions under a dome of emotional distancing, no light or love can get in or out of our hearts; bitterness grows within its darkened recesses.

Without the stimulation of positive or negative emotional responses, we begin to atrophy, much as our muscles do without sufficient exercise or use. We weaken our bodies and cripple our minds with a victim mentality, forgetting that we were created with a spirit of strength and victory, of light and love.

We cannot always predict when or how our emotions will be affected by the ups and downs of daily living; we can, however, control how we respond to life's uncertainties. We can choose to seek the light, no matter how difficult the situation, knowing that even the darkest of nights eventually ends with a glorious sunrise and the gift of a new dawn!

Slice of Time

I once heard it said that it only takes twelve minutes out of an entire day of activities for someone to determine whether their day was good or bad.

According to the theory, only twelve minutes of negative input, activity, or otherwise-unpleasant experiences in a day can produce a negative attitude about whether the day was good or bad.

Perhaps even more interesting is that it didn't matter whether the adverse reaction was the result of a series of unrelated events during the day, adding up to twelve minutes, or if it was the product of a single twelve-minute blast of negative disruption. The result was the same; twelve minutes of negative experience produced the same conclusion about that day.

To allow ourselves to be influenced so profoundly by such a small slice of daily living seems to devalue most of our thoughts, breaths, and other moments in our day, or, for that matter, in our lives.

While twelve minutes of disruption may seem too short an interval on which to shape our attitude for the day, it is certain that just one moment of brokenheartedness colors our day as profoundly as the cream in our morning coffee, changing the tone and texture, and influencing our ability to fully enjoy the present.

However, we have within us a spirit of strength and endurance to overcome the moments of disruption, anger, disappointment, and heartbreak. We need only to summon that spirit.

Time Sensitive

Each of us is a special person. We are all given the chance in our lives to fill ourselves with great love for those around us. If we choose to take advantage of it, we may sacrifice our health and sanity by tending to the needs of others, no matter how tired we may be or how much we might have already done.

How can this be? The seeds of greatness that have been planted within us have flourished; they have roots of divine origin.

I reflect on the sacrifices I've made in my life and the hardships I've endured, some self-imposed and others just a matter of chance. I feel the pain of loss, as I am human. I recognize the tightening in my belly as I face each new day with uncertainty about what might confront me. I pause during the day in moments of reflection, amid thoughts of inadequacy for the tasks of the day, as well as the challenges of life.

I crawl into bed each night and exhale a breath of release, but also of thanksgiving. I cannot control all the pieces of my existence or the surprises I will encounter along my life's journey, but I can control my reactions to the twists and turns and the new realities I face along the way.

I can also cultivate my awareness of who I am and how far I have come on my journey, including how much I have grown and how many others I have helped and loved along the way.

We are forever growing, changing, loving, and deeming ourselves and others worthy of kindness. When we fully realize this truth and take advantage of the opportunities presented to us each day, we can climb into our beds each evening with aching muscles and exhausted minds, knowing that we have lived up to our potential and purpose that day. We can then fall asleep with a smile of accomplishment on our face and a prayer of thanksgiving on our lips.

Number the Heroes

Over the past few years, our reality has been shaped and changed in many ways. Pandemics, inflation, the wars in Ukraine and the Middle East, border security… The list goes on and on.

Each of us has been awakened to the new normal. Though the final shape is still to be determined, we already know that this rock upon which we spin through space will be forever changed. The question remains whether that change will be for the better or just another missed opportunity for humanity to grow beyond its current state of self-centered indulgence.

While many still suffer from illnesses brought on by the viruses of the body and the spirit, there are signs of hope and growth amid the ashes and tears. Each of us has a story to tell and a unique perspective on a new understanding of our connection to one another. We are reminded daily that each of us has a responsibility for and a dependency on each other.

While we may choose to put on a mask of protection from the virus infecting our bodies, we can protect our spirits by embracing the reality of our interconnected nature as singular threads in the fabric of humanity. As each day presents new challenges to our understanding of our routines and responsibilities, we get glimpses of victories on our journey towards a shared destiny.

We are encouraged by the stories of dedication and tireless efforts of healthcare workers who minister to those in overwhelmed hospitals and ICUs. We find strength and hope in the commitment of those in authority to provide a safe environment for each of us, to protect us from our vulnerability. We now see new value in the previously invisible services and activities of everyday life. We find hope in the random acts of kindness of strangers and family, whether long known or newly acquired.

While we may still be searching for remedies to our warring egoes and the viral ills of our bodies, the formula for treating our ailing spirits is quite clear. Each of us can become a hero to someone in need. The question is, how many of us will respond to the call?

Empathetic Awakenings

Author Bob Bullard wrote, "The highest form of knowledge is empathy, for it requires us to suspend our egos and live in another's world." This observation rings true for those of us who are open to the uncomfortable realities found in the lives of those who pass by us each day.

Like wisps of wind, those unknown faces race by us—some with eyes full and bright with expectation, and others with eyes empty and devoid of the simplest of dreams. They approach; they pause; then they pass by in silence to most ears, except for the few attuned to the tones of despair and the callings of an aching heart.

The pace of our steps further shortens our opportunity to capture even the thinnest of exchanges of mind and heart, bound as we are to the pursuit of our daily rituals and to our covenant with the familiarities of our lives and the paths we follow.

With good intentions, we strive to reach our fullest emotional potential. However, life demands that we continually move forward on our journey and encourage, even for the briefest of moments, those who stand still. Often, before we fully grasp the opportunity to intercede in the lives of those who weep in the darkness and yet summon the courage to move forward into their uncertainties, we have already passed one another, having found our stride and a direction unique to the current realities of our existence.

No matter how we might try, we cannot fit into the shoes of another, nor can we walk the exact steps of another's journey in life. Those shoes and their path are unique to them. We can only wear the shoes and walk the path that best fits our own journey and connects us to a spirit and a consciousness we share with all those whom we meet along the way. As if they are rivers flowing through and around all of us, healing and hope surround us and are there for all who make themselves available to be cleansed by their transformational powers.

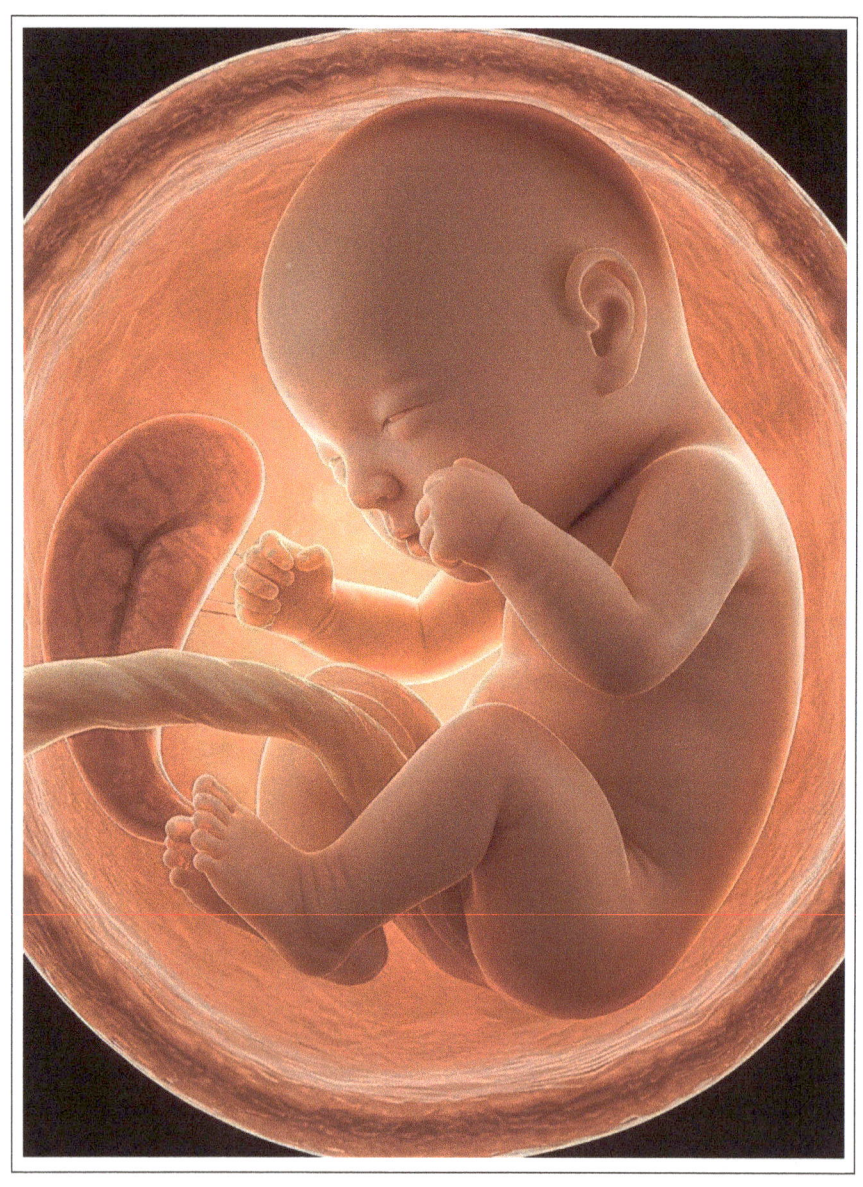

First Day of Forever

Life is forever changing. Where we begin our journey and where it ends might be the same, but everything that we see, touch, and feel in between is constantly changing. Each day, the reality of the world in which we live is being redefined.

We, too, are not immune to change; each day, we rediscover who we are and what drives us onward. Maslow's hierarchy of needs notwithstanding, each of us stretches the reality we confront each day to fit our passions and the purpose of our steps.

Like riding the current in an ever-flowing river of unfamiliar twists and turns, we move forward without conscious thought of our direction. We travel from moments of hurried pace and frantic responses to quiet pools of reflection, allowing us a glimpse of our surroundings and of who we are at that exact point on our journey.

An unseen, unrelenting current pushes us forward as we draw closer to our destiny; we are unaware of what lies ahead and of the form life will take as we navigate unfamiliar and changing waters. While we may move left or right through each turn, and while our pace may slow or quicken, we are all compelled, by the unstoppable rhythm of our lives, to press onward.

What we see around us as we navigate the uncertainties of our journey will shape our thinking. Like our surroundings, our view of life changes with each turn as shadows grow and deepen, and the light of the day creates new images of forgotten memories. Once again, we experience emotions and attitudes we had set aside due to the demands of our daily routines; they are different now… because we are different.

Our view of the world changes as we move through life because life changes for each of us. What we saw and experienced as we set out on our singular journey is different from what we see and experience today because we are different. The twists and turns, surprises, and disappointments we have confronted along the way have all helped to shape the reality we experience each day of our travels.

While we may view our world differently as we make our way towards our destiny, our hope and our endeavor is that with each passing day, we can find still waters and that the reflection we see in the stillness is one of acceptance and love for ourselves and for each other.

First Rule of Holes

Occasionally, each of us comes across a word, a phrase, or an utterance that seems to perfectly fit the occasion or situation in life that we find ourselves dealing with at that moment. When it happens, it may evoke a hearty laugh from us or possibly a tear or a moment of reflection. Regardless, we set aside those words and the associated memories, as arrows in our emotional quiver, to be used repeatedly later.

Several years ago, I stumbled across a saying called The First Rule of Holes. The saying goes something like this: "The first rule of holes is that when you are in one, stop digging!"

When I first read or heard that saying, it could instantly be applied to any number of issues or situations with which I was dealing at that time. I could never imagine just how many more times in my life I would be reaching back into my quiver to draw out once again that specific arrow. There seems to be no limit to the mistakes that one person can make in their life or on the number of times needed to remind oneself that if you have dug yourself into a hole, then at the very least, don't make it bigger.

Each morning, we may rise anxiously, waiting to surf the wormholes of our lives—those sudden moments when we are at the exactly right time and place in life for our emotional and physical needs to intersect with those of another—that transform both us and those around us. To me, the essence of finding passion in life lies in the uncertainties created by intersecting lives and emotions. While each occurrence may produce passion, there is no guarantee of a specific result; we may continue to dig into the emptiness of the resulting outcome, or we may put down our shovels, having uncovered something of great value, and no longer need to dig deeper.

Such a moment came to me many years ago. At that time, I was struggling with the broken pieces of an even more severely broken relationship. It wasn't the first time, but that fact didn't make the situation any easier or the pain of loss any less. To make matters worse, I was experiencing all of this just before the holiday season; there was ample opportunity for me to consider the feelings of loneliness and disappointment as I faced the prospects of "decking the halls" on my own, a kind of Folly Jolly Christmas of sorts.

During that time, I ran into some old friends whom I hadn't seen for many years. They invited me to attend a church service with them on Sunday. It was their church, somewhere I had never been, and I didn't know anyone other than these two friends. They invited me to join them in worship and then for brunch at their home afterwards.

It was a thoughtful gesture, and I needed both the worship and the company, so I happily accepted the invitation.

That Sunday, we gathered in the church, finding seats near the front and center. We shared prayers and meditation and listened to the thoughtful sermon by the minister, to whom I had been introduced before the service. Sitting to my left were my two friends, eyes closed in silent prayer and meditation. To my right was an elderly woman, also with her eyes closed. The minister had called for a moment of silence, after which he asked us to turn to one another and offer a greeting.

I first turned to my left, offering a greeting to both of my old friends and accepting their good wishes. Then I turned to my right, but before I could offer a greeting to the elderly woman next to me, she reached out and took my hand. She looked into my eyes and softly said, "You have a hole in your heart, but don't worry; God is going to fill it."

I had never seen that woman before, and I never saw her again. The two friends with whom I had attended the church service and had brunch disappeared into the background, and I never saw them again either.

A few weeks later, I received an invitation from a casual friend who asked if I would be interested in joining her for a play in town. It seems that a customer of hers had given my friend two tickets that they could not use. I had no plans for that night, so I accepted the invitation.

That night was nearly ten years ago. I didn't know it at the time, but that evening would be the start of a wonderful and enduring relationship with a very special woman who shares many of the same values. Faith, love of family, travel, the exquisite simplicity of a fire, a glass of wine, and good music—we enjoy them together as we travel through life with all its ups, downs, and uncertainties. My Irish step-dancing girl and I are going strong.

Each morning, as I begin my day with prayer and praise to my Creator, I thank Him for filling the hole in my heart as He had promised. I look for opportunities to minister to the needs of others, especially those whose hearts may need mending.

Maybe now—or before the holiday season or amid the present global folly—is a good time to look to our left and right and find those unknown friends who have hearts in need of mending, who have holes in their hearts in need of filling. Offer them the comfort and assurance that they can stop digging and, instead, accept the gift of healing that is waiting for them as long as they have the faith and resolve to believe it to be so.

Awaken, Oh Peaceful Heart

A peaceful heart knows no age or status in life; it has no memory of past failures or unrealized dreams. It obeys no boundaries for sharing or limits to loving another.

A peaceful heart finds no comfort in the pain of others nor recoils in condescending pretense to the cries of the poor, the lonely, and those in need of love and support. It finds its reflection in the longing hearts of others and seeks residence in the quiet corners of a contemplative and accepting mind.

A peaceful heart willingly combines all these qualities and actions into a fabric of many threads, a patchwork of many colors, textures, and visions that enfolds all of us without exception or judgment.

It is the realization that we make a difference in this life—one heart, one mind at a time—if we dare to let it be so!

Shifting Sands

Life presents us all with challenges. Sometimes, these challenges are simple and require little from us, other than minor adjustments in our habits or thinking. Other challenges may demand more from us, forcing us to look more deeply into our hearts and minds to reshape our view of either ourselves or the world around us, or sometimes both.

Whatever the case, as we move down our selected paths in life, we settle into the rituals of daily living, sometimes forgetting about the simpler challenges presented to us. At other times, we are consumed with the weight of the obstacles in front of us, and we can barely recognize the people and activities around us, focusing instead on the size of our challenge.

The clock of life ticks forward for each of us at the same measured rate, but how we live each moment determines how much joy we can squeeze into whatever number of days and breaths we have left on this twisting stone that we call home.

Suppose we focus our attention on the part of our journey still ahead of us. In that case, we will quickly realize that the number of days before us is dwarfed by the memories and reflections of days already counted, and we can become frozen in that realization. In so doing, our focus in life is then narrowed to counting days and breaths instead of focusing on the real challenge of living: our ability to share and bring love into our lives and the lives of others.

It's been said that relying on the world around us to give us peace is akin to gazing at a picture of food and expecting to feel full. As we have the responsibility to nourish our bodies with food that sustains us healthily, we also have the responsibility to take control of our lives and direct our thoughts and activities towards honing our spiritual and emotional well-being.

Counting hours and breaths is much more tedious and unfulfilling than counting smiles and hearty laughs. While there is a limit on how much reflective thinking is healthy for each of us, there is no limit to the amount of joy with which we can fill our hearts if we dare to focus on the good that is yet to be in our lives!

Addictive Personality
For Ed

Each Memorial Day, we remember those who put their country, their faith, or their families before themselves and moved on to their shared destiny.

My brother was one of those people. While I still remember celebrating his birthday, which came just a few days before my own, I also remember with greater depth his passing just a few years ago. He was a brother, a husband, a son, an uncle, and a friend. It seems much longer than just a few spins around our star since he left us. So much has changed in our world since his passing, yet many things have remained the same.

While it was a failing from dementia that took down this warrior, many have been felled by a virus with an all-too-familiar name and number during that same period. They were brothers, fathers, sons, husbands, uncles, and friends as well. While my brother had a unique and undeniable personality, he shared many things with those countless others who made their way ashore over those difficult years.

A love of family and faith, a deep and abiding joy in expressing that faith, a passion for meeting people and for experiencing the beauty in this world—these were the things that drove my brother and his fellow travelers to make a lasting impression on our hearts and minds.

Most of all, we were privileged to witness their insatiable desire to make the world a better place. Whether doing it on a grand scale for all of the world to see, hovering over the sick beside a hospital bed, standing guard on a wall to watch over us, or perhaps whispering in the ear of someone needing to feel loved or included as they battled an addiction or other challenge, they all yearned to make a difference.

So as each Memorial Day comes upon us, let us remember not only the bravery and sacrifice of our men and women in military uniform, but also the sacrifice of those among us, regardless of age, sex, faith, color, or sexual preference, who gave so freely of themselves and their lives so that others could find a brighter day and an easier road in moving towards their destinies.

Altered States

The unpredictable pendulum of chance has me once again chasing my memories of cacti, camels, piñons, and friends old and still as I return to a place and a time once filled with so many dreams.

I find myself back in a place that once filled me with the visions only experienced by one who is confronted by the tugs and pulls of maturation, the same place where I found, over the desert hills, little sprinklings of possibilities scattered like expectant seeds yearning to drink from the fountain of a young man's desires.

While destiny would have its way with my desert dreams, and I would find these hills and valleys void of the kind of fulfillment I had imagined, I sustained my spirit beneath the unrelenting sun by listening in the quiet of the desert hills for the breath of our Creator.

With distance for reflection and the realization of the inevitable change that accompanies time and perspective, I return to the desert hills and to the memories of what could have been, to find a new set of possibilities yet to be explored.

I no longer brood over things denied me so many years ago. Instead, I celebrate what is to be enjoyed in the present, and I indulge myself in the memories of what the future may hold for me.

The breath of God still echoes in between the cactus and the sage and all through the canyons of my mind. Unlike me, the desert remains unchanged.

As Kindness Does
(For Cece)

I was taking a walk this morning when I passed a woman wearing a T-shirt with Try Kindness printed on the front. It struck me as something obvious yet so easily overlooked in our everyday interactions with others.

When I got home, I was catching up on my social media posts, and one of those frequent social media memories came up. It was a picture of my disabled son and the young woman who was our waitress at a restaurant where we had dined a few weeks earlier.

What struck me then—and still brings a smile to my face—is how that young woman completely overlooked the wheelchair in which my son sat, as well as his apparent physical disabilities. She instead went about her business as usual, focusing on my son's personality and his willingness to show friendship, as well as on our dinner orders. Since that time, we have all remained friends on social media, sharing our victories and disappointments with open and accepting hearts and minds.

It's just a reminder that what is printed on our shirts and what we say aren't nearly as important as what we do for others and what is in our hearts.

Forgotten Moments

One evening, while going through some old photographs, I came across some black-and-white pictures of my mom and dad when they were young and newly married. It reminded me of the unseen history that each of us has as we view the lives of our parents before we were born through the lens of our receding years.

It's easy to forget that many of our parents were much the same in their youth as we are in ours, enjoying the moments in between disruptions, dressing up and feeling good about life at that given moment, smiling, and taking pleasure in each other's company.

Their time may have passed, but their words about "enjoying life while the flame still burns" echo in my ears. Another birthday completed. Another morning has arrived along with the opportunity to make a difference in the world by bringing a bit of hope, joy, and love to all whom we meet on this day…to change the world, one heart, one smile at a time!

Back to the Garden

The famous physicist and cosmologist Carl Sagan once said that "dust is the currency of the cosmos, and mathematics is its language." While this statement attempts to explain our universe and our existence in quantifiable terms, it is incomplete at best.

Regardless of the lens through which we observe the cosmos at its grandest scale or the intricacies of the nearly invisible quantum world, we can never see more than a tiny part of the complete picture of creation and our existence.

While we may not yet have enough insight to explain the physical world around us adequately, we can accept its existence by acknowledging that on our own, we are little more than handfuls of stardust set into motion, and it is in this spirit that we become fearless servants of our Creator's will, destined to shine brighter than any star in the heavens.

Secret Place

There's a bridge that straddles our secret place; it spans all our lives with an unspoken grace. From end to end, its creaky bones stretch, in silence, still able our memories to fetch.

Weathered days pass us by, both of joy and of dread, patiently waiting for the days still ahead. Each heartbeat connected, together as one, our twisting stone circles a more distant sun.

The days grow colder, rushing by much too fast, barely time to remember the dreams of the past. Eyes looking upward, open wide in the dimming light, we celebrate our victory and prepare to take flight.

Connecting the past to our shared destiny, each step brings us closer to what we must be. Our spirits to travel as partners through time, our journey completed, companions forever, we fly!

About Being Authentic

Sometimes I get lost in my memories, in the words I put to life, and I start thinking about possibilities and what it means to be an "authentic" person. I think about how much I enjoy people and about being in a loving relationship with a special person, even if just for a portion of my days on this twisting stone.

I close my eyes and dream of how wonderful it feels to fall asleep each night beside the person I love, and how comforting it is to put my arms around the woman who loves me, at least in equal measure, for just being who I am, despite all my shortcomings. I lie beside her in bed, hoping that she knows that I am also beside her in life, with equal enthusiasm and commitment.

I stop dreaming and gather myself; I remember that personal integrity is an essential part of the formula for both balance and peace in our lives, and how it is an integral part of a loving relationship. Integrity drives us to consider our responsibilities, commitments, and choices in all aspects of our lives.

If we strive to become people of high integrity, we can't help but become more authentic. In this process, we open ourselves to the fullness of life and the peace that comes with being true to our spiritual nature. I reflect on the special people in my life—my family and friends—and how important it is to pause and appreciate these relationships. As true friendship is unbounded by distance or time, the embodiment of authenticity is simply friendship in action and a benevolence and sincerity towards all those with whom we interact and in all that we do!

Illumination

In the vast cosmic dance of time and space, a quest for meaning, the human race. From dawn's first light to twilight's embrace, we ponder the essence, the purpose we chase.

What lies beyond this mortal shore? A riddle as old as existence's core. In nature's symphony, we yearn to explore. The elusive answer, forevermore.

Is life a fleeting breath, a weary sigh? A mere interlude before we say goodbye? Or is it a tapestry, colors that fly, threads woven together as the moments pass by?

In the gentle whispers of a summer breeze or the roaring waves of mighty seas, in the laughter of children, their innocent ease, we catch a glimpse of the echoes of life's mysteries.

Life's true meaning lies not in name, material wealth, or transient fame. It blooms in compassion, in love's sacred flame, in kind acts and virtues, our souls to reclaim.

So embrace the beauty of each fleeting day, and find solace in moments that quietly unfold. Seek truth in the stars as they eternally play, and let gratitude guide your heart on the way.

For when our journey's complete and the shadows descend, the true meaning of life will be found in the end, in the echoes of hearts healed by love, and in the blessings we've shared, our gifts from above.

In thanksgiving and grace, our spirits are humbled; under the light of brotherhood, we shall not stumble. Instead, we can dance without regrets, no reason for sorrow. Just joy, peace, and wonder as we look towards tomorrow.

So let us dance in harmony with all the unknowns, with open hearts and spirits, forever grown, embracing the wonders life has shown, for in the meaning we seek, we are never alone!

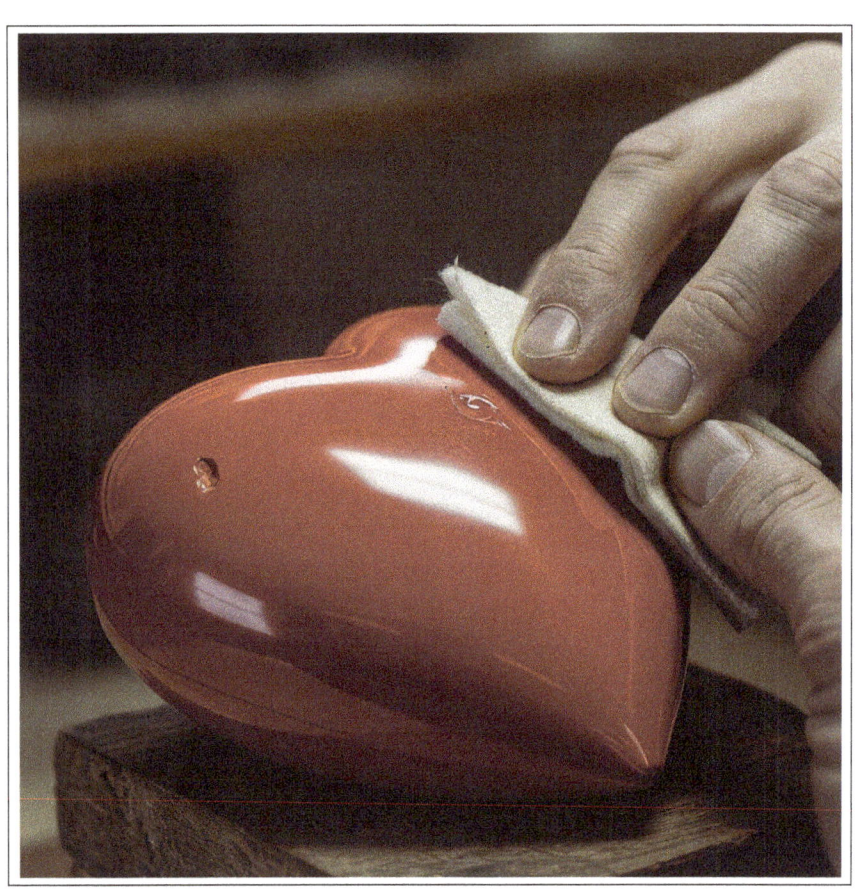

Renews the Heart

I've always found the celebration of Valentine's Day to be a curious contradiction of sorts. On the one hand, much time and resources are spent looking for an appropriate way to express love, if not commitment, to those whom we hold dear. On the other hand, we struggle through tortured hours of reflection as we look back over our relationships with questions, uneasy memories, and self-reflection.

For those who see February 14 as an opportunity to indulge in romance, it provides an immediate rush of sweet bliss, setting our hearts on fire, our pulses racing, and our minds careening between hopeful thoughts and secret wishes.

Like the icing on a cake, there is no denying the allure of romance when we happen upon it; its call on our hearts is unmistakable. But real substance and enduring satisfaction are found beneath the icing, beneath the romance. It is found in the underlying love upon which romance must be built.

What we put into the cake batter, what we put into our hearts, determines the shape and form of the final product. Neither icing nor romance alone is self-sustaining. Both must be renewed periodically to remain current.

Our true joy and satisfaction are best served, though, when we can experience both the sweetness of romance as well as the fullness of love. Some may argue that romance and love are two separate and unrelated things, that love is not a prerequisite for enjoying the thrill of romantic experiences.

It would be difficult to argue against the notion that romance is separate and distinct from love. After all, we can love our children, our friends, even our pets, without any need or requirement on our part for a romantic connection.

But just as Einstein described entangled particles as "spooky action at a distance," the feeling of romance and the emotion of love are connected in ways only observed in the quiet recesses of the wanting heart. Why then must we confine our demonstration of love and the joy of romantic connection to the twelfth day after Groundhog Day?

Each spin of the stone upon which we ride provides us with the opportunity to refresh our commitments to one another, some with romantic bliss and others with a reaffirmation and a renewal of love, but all falling upon waiting hearts.

Guiding Light

It's been said that guidance is whispers of light that shine through life's darkness, illuminating the way to one's highest good. I like that!

The more we trust the guidance from the Spirit within us, the more confident we become in knowing how to live out each day of our lives and how to transform these whispers into a life of service to others and meaning for ourselves.

While each of us may have been given different talents, capabilities, and seeds of greatness, no matter who we are or what the earthly circumstances may be in our lives, our value as a member of this divine brotherhood is measured by how much we share of what has been sown into our spirit.

Tender Moment

As I make my way down the twisting road that is life, even after more than sixty years on this spinning stone, it never ceases to amaze me how unprepared I still am for life's many surprises.

While this holds for me in many areas, it has proven exceptionally accurate when it comes to anticipating how, when, and where romance will develop in my life. I find myself woefully inadequate when trying to gauge when Cupid's arrows will find their way into my throbbing heart and render me hopelessly in love.

One grey November morning, I made my way into the airport terminal from the parking garage, anticipating yet another business trip and what had become a routinely boring travel assignment. At least the parking garage wasn't full this time; I was traveling a full three days before the Thanksgiving holiday, beating the crush of airport activity by at least one full day.

I made my way along what had become my practiced and preferred route through the airport terminal, towards my departure gate. No surprises today, same departure gate again. You would think that whoever schedules these gate assignments would want to mix it up a little every once in a while, making it more interesting for travelers and more difficult for potential terrorists to plan their diabolical deeds.

Onward, past the Starbucks boutique, around the corner, and down the walkway, passing the bookstore, glancing at the display of new hardcover treasures…same books as last week. Everything seemed as diffused and grey as the overcast sky hanging above the runway, another dull grey day, another dull grey trip…no surprises.

As I made my way around the last turn on this all-too-familiar route, I saw her. At first, it was just a glance, a fleeting glimpse of her in between the interruptions from the constant parade of people moving through the area. Yes, it was she. I knew that face. I knew that form. I had studied that smile many times before as I passed her in the airport and wondered what had brought her to this place and how comfortable she looked talking with people—more relaxed than I, for sure, as I had never been able to summon the courage to engage her in conversation when I had run into her in the past.

She was beautiful—dark skin, slender build, and definitely of Spanish origin. Her long raven curls bounced back and forth as if they belonged to an exotic dancer hoping to excite those who followed her seductive movements. Her eyes were wide and bright, like polished onyx, and they moved playfully beneath her long, soft eyelashes. Yes, I had studied her in the past. I knew her voice was wispy and throaty, a seductive combination. Her lips were full and beautifully outlined her mouth, turned up so slightly at each corner. She was exquisite.

Never had she even given the slightest clue that she had taken note of me. So many others were more worthy of her attention; why would I think that today was different? I once again resigned myself to the same results, the same routine travel, and the same grey November gloom.

Then, as if by some divine intervention, the rush of bodies through the terminal swept me up in its flow and quite unexpectedly deposited me directly in front of this woman whom I had admired for so long, but only from a distance. I now stood just a few feet from her. I could easily read the name tag she was wearing; her name was Serena.

"Good morning." She smiled at me.

"Hello," I responded, then continued, "kind of busy here today."

"Yes, it is, but I've been waiting just for you," Serena replied.

What was happening? In all my dreams and all my well-played scenarios, I had never imagined that I would be standing here in front of this woman, let alone have her tell me that she had been waiting for me. Maybe she had noticed me at the airport in the past. Perhaps she was as shy and uncertain as I was, unwilling to risk the first advance, content to dream of what might be.

Gathering myself, I stood erect, raising my eyes to meet hers. There seemed to be some form of unspoken exchange between us as she moved closer to me, close enough that I could lose myself in the intoxicating scent of her perfume, close enough that I could feel her breath on my face. She was even more enchanting at this close distance.

Then, unexpectedly, she reached for me, found my arm, and pulled me forward towards her. She moved her right hand to my shoulder and gently let it ride down the curve of my back, then quickly moved it away in some playful ritual.

I was speechless. I had never experienced such a rush, such a tingle up and down my spine. I felt myself becoming aroused. But she seemed intent on finishing what she had started and drew me closer still. She deftly moved her hands down my sides and onto my thighs.

I could barely contain myself. I felt that I would explode with just one more whiff of her fragrance. Surely, I would cry out in ecstasy if she continued to move her hands up and down my inner thighs.

Suddenly, she looked deep into my eyes with a fixed and purposeful expression on her face. Gently, she removed her hands from where they had silently felt all that this man could be, all that I hoped I could be. I froze for a moment, trying to understand what just happened, trying to anticipate what was next.

She backed away slightly, a bit flushed in the cheeks. She held herself still, no more raven hair dancing, and in a more formal and practiced voice, she looked into my eyes one last time and said, "Have a nice trip."

Still riveted to this woman and wondering about the significance of what had just happened, I watched her as she turned away, leaving me with my mouth open and in awe of this public interlude.

Time to move on; my dream, though brief, was finally realized beyond any expectation. Glancing over my shoulder to savor one last view of this dream come true, I could clearly see the monogram on the back of her blouse and easily read TSA; the pat-down was complete. I successfully made it through security.

Now, on to my plane!

Uncertain Reality
A Matter of Quantum Spirituality

Imagine a universe that keeps going and going with no edges or ends. The concept of an "infinite universe" is difficult to envision because we typically think of things having limits. If the universe is truly infinite, it raises many questions. Could there be other kinds of life out there? Are there endless versions of things happening across this vast space? It's hard to believe that the universe might not have a beginning or an end. It makes you think!

Considering a God who is infinite or without limits is also distinct from our conventional religious ideas. An infinite God would have no limits to power or knowledge and would have always existed. Considering a God like this prompts us to wonder why the universe is the way it is and what our purpose is in this vast scheme. It also makes us wonder whether we make our own choices or if God already predetermined everything.

Quantum theory, on the other hand, is about the tiniest parts of the universe, like atoms and even more minute stuff. One weird idea is "superposition." This means that these little bits can be in many places or states at the same time until we look at them. Another strange idea, the "uncertainty principle" proposed by Werner Heisenberg, states that we can't know both exactly where a tiny particle is and how fast it's moving at the same time. These ideas differ from how we perceive things working in our everyday lives. They demonstrate that the basic level of reality is highly unpredictable.

What's interesting is that all three of these ideas—an infinite universe, an infinite God, and quantum theory—are full of mystery. We can't fully understand any of them, and they push the limits of what our brains can grasp. Just as we can't imagine something that never ends, the weirdness of quantum theory also feels like a great mystery.

These three ideas might even be connected. If the universe continues forever, it might make the idea of a God who also endures seem more plausible. A universe that big might have needed a power beyond what we can understand to create it. Additionally, quantum theory suggests that observing something can alter its state. This makes us wonder if our minds and awareness contribute to shaping reality.

The concepts of a universe that never ends, a God without limits, and the strange rules of quantum theory make us think hard about what it means to be alive, what we can and can't know, and how the biggest things in the universe might be connected to the smallest. These ideas, when combined, create a sense of mystery about the universe that inspires us to continue exploring what reality is truly like.

An infinite universe makes us think that there could be other life out there, besides us. This makes us wonder if humans are truly that special and prompts us to consider all the various forms of life that could exist in space. It might even alter how we perceive our significance in the universe.

The concept of an infinite God prompts us to consider a being that isn't limited by time or space. This prompts us to ask why things were created, if there is a plan for everything, and how everything in the universe might be interconnected. If this idea aligns with the concept of an infinite universe, it suggests that this plan could be unfolding everywhere in it.

In the end, contemplating an infinite universe, an infinite God, and the mysteries of quantum theory reveals a complex web of ideas that prompts us to think, inspires us to learn more, and motivates us to continue asking questions. These ideas help us gain a better understanding of our place in the universe and encourage us to explore the deep mysteries of existence with curiosity, recognizing that there are probably endless things we still don't know… and may never know.

Even though science, religion, and quantum theory are different ways of looking at reality, the concepts of an infinite universe, an infinite God, and the peculiar aspects of quantum physics all reveal that there are limits to our understanding. But we are no strangers to the unknown, so we move forward one idea, one experiment, one piece of existence at a time.

We nurture our collective ignorance; we celebrate our gained insights; we deepen our faith in what we cannot fully understand. It is as much in our shared unknowing as it is in our discoveries that we find our connections with one another and to our shared destiny.

Cosmic Threads
Connecting in an Infinite Universe

L ife presents many unknowns. Every sunrise offers both possibilities and new experiences. We are required to navigate our journey through life, determining the pace and direction of our progress.

We may decide to step forward cautiously, electing to measure our progress along the way with periods of reflection and reassessment, or we may throw ourselves into life with reckless abandon, challenging its passion and purpose. Whatever our choice, our destiny is realized with each step we take.

Whether we choose to move forward into the light of each new day and confront life on our terms, or we choose to hide in the shadows, waiting to be discovered by it, we are pulled forward on our journey one day at a time.

We may venture forward with eyes closed to soften the ugly wrinkles of life, or perhaps we choose to greet each new day with eyes wide open, hoping to take in every bit of light from each sunrise, measuring our journey one wrinkle at a time and anticipating every unborn memory. Either way, no two steps of our trip will ever be the same, nor will they ever again be walked in quite the same way.

Life calls us into action. Every success or failure and each challenge provides us with an opportunity to grow beyond our self-imposed limitations, but only if we can transform our thinking as we move forward on our life journey. That requires us to learn how to forgive ourselves when we make mistakes, to forgive others when their actions and decisions conflict with our own, and, lastly, to learn from all our experiences.

Each step we take on our path through life and each person we meet along the way is unique, as are we. Where we end up on our journey is determined by the strength of our character and how successful we are in refining it with the universal tools of faith, learning, commitment, and willing self-examination.

There is no work life or home life; there is just life, measured in breaths and heartbeats, colored by our experiences. If we are wise and attend to our personal growth with knowledge and a spirit of connection, then our journey will be one of joy, regardless of the underlying circumstances. Instead of spending our remaining days counting each step of our trip, we can fall asleep each night counting our treasured moments, our best experiences, and our blessings!

Reality Check

Cultural Realism and Ultimate Truth

Imagine different groups of friends, each with their inside jokes and ways of doing things. What is funny to one group might not make sense to another. That's "cultural realism." It's the idea that what you consider normal, correct, or even accurate depends on your specific culture. One culture might value being very direct, while another might think that's impolite or disrespectful. Cultural realism suggests that both ways are acceptable *within their own cultures*. It means there isn't just one single "right" way for everyone to live or see things.

Now, think about something like gravity. It doesn't matter if you're in the United States, China, or Australia—if you drop something, it falls. Some people believe that there are truths, such as the law of gravity, that are universally true, regardless of one's culture. This concept is known as the "ultimate truth." It's the idea that there's an absolute, unchanging truth out there that exists even if people disagree on it. Think of it like a universal rule or a fundamental reality.

So how do these two ideas fit together? It can get a little tricky. If different cultures have different ideas about what's true and correct, how can there be one single ultimate truth for everyone? It almost sounds as if they can't both be correct.

But some people think they *can* work together. Maybe the ultimate truth is like a diamond with many different facets. Each culture sees a different side of the diamond, and they all have a valid perspective even though it's not the whole picture. Another idea is that perhaps our concept of ultimate truth itself is something our own culture has invented.

What's the big deal? Essentially, cultural realism asserts that different cultures perceive the world differently, and that's okay. The ultimate truth assumes there's a real, unchanging truth out there for everyone.

The relationship between these two ideas has been a topic of discussion for a long time. There's no easy answer. It prompts us to consider what truth truly means, how much our culture influences our beliefs, and whether there are limits to what we can know.

Considering cultural realism and ultimate truth can help us see the world as diverse and having various perspectives, while also raising questions about a possible shared reality. Connecting internally and externally with others may bridge gaps between different interpretations of reality and truth.

Viewing our collective experiences as individual threads in the fabric of existence allows us to value diverse opinions that add dimension to this fabric without altering its fundamental purpose.

Ultimately, considering cultural realism and the pursuit of ultimate truth helps us understand that the world is a diverse place with many ways of perceiving things; it also prompts us to wonder if there is a deeper shared reality beyond our comprehension.

Brown-Eyed Girl

Passion—now there's a word that pirouettes at the center of every memorable story. Some insist passion is the secret ingredient that transforms the ordinary into the unforgettable, that rare elixir that colors our days with a vibrancy not found in any paintbox. Sure, we can mosey through life grumbling about our coworkers, the quirks of our families, or the way the toaster always burns one side of the bread. We're experts at cataloging imperfections, especially those that belong to ourselves. But let's be honest: that's the easy route, and it seldom leads to anything worth remembering.

We don't get to shuffle the cards we're handed in this strange game called life. But—ah!—we do decide how to play them. And the way we play, the spirit we bring to each turn, is written in bold ink by the things we care deeply about. Passion is not just the fuel in our tank; it's the turbocharge that makes the drive worthwhile, revving our engines as we speed toward moments that linger in memory long after the road has ended.

You might ask, Where does passion hide? Is it waiting at the top of the Great Wall of China, nestled among monks greeting dawn with whispered prayers, or hurtling around a racetrack strapped into a 700-horsepower beast, heart thumping in your throat? Certainly, those experiences jolt us awake, but I'd argue that passion is just as likely to ambush us in the everyday: a shared glance across a crowded street, a heated debate over morning coffee, or a late-night conversation that meanders far past midnight.

For me, passion pulses through the little things—each interaction a flickering candle illuminating the vast, interconnected tapestry of our lives. The world spins, and we're all fellow passengers, linked by stardust and a shared journey through the quirks of existence.

Traveling to far-flung corners of the globe is a tried-and-true way to rattle the snow globe of routine, stirring up the possibility of new friends, new ideas, and those delightful moments of discomfort that lead us to grow. Yet, the most transformative journeys are often those we take close to home, in the unscripted interactions and serendipitous discoveries of daily life.

My own career has been a passport to the world, introducing me to a constellation of fascinating souls—some met in bustling airports, others in the quiet hum of online spaces like LinkedIn or the organized chaos of Facebook. Each encounter, each conversation, is a thread pulled from the fabric of passion, adding color and complexity to the tapestry of my experience.

Growing up in the 1950s, in a small university town, I learned early that the world contained multitudes.

Wandering the campus streets, a cacophony of languages serenaded me, the sizzle of foreign spices mixing in the air, and the rhythmic shuffle of footsteps echoing dreams from every corner of the globe. The city felt like a living mosaic, flecked with history and possibility.

No autumn stroll beneath the red-gold trees, nor any lesson learned beneath ivy-covered arches, could have prepared me for the whirlwind of adventure awaiting on the Asian subcontinent. It was only after two decades of steady work that I found myself—somewhat reluctantly at first—boarding a plane bound for India, anxiety and anticipation squabbling over the armrest. Sixteen hours in a flying tin can, wedged between strangers vying for turf, hardly felt like the start of a passionate escapade, yet that's where the magic began.

Even the most routine rituals—like handing off my keys to the airport valet on a drizzly November evening—hold the potential for discovery if you know where to look. I've learned that opportunities for passion, transformation, and sheer delight are everywhere, scattered like confetti across our ordinary days. Sometimes, they arrive disguised as mysterious strangers in airport terminals, as fleeting as a glance and as unforgettable as a song you can't get out of your head.

So off I went, once again, back to the embrace of Mother India—a place that had become both a second home and a proving ground for passion, resilience, and the joy of connection.

Let me paint you a picture: a 10:00 PM east coast departure, with a two-hour layover in Abu Dhabi thrown in for good measure, and a total of eighteen glorious hours of travel—in other words, just enough time to question every life choice that led you to this moment. Toss in a ten-and-a-half-hour time difference, and voilà, you stagger into New Delhi at a crisp 1:30 AM, two days later, wondering if you've accidentally time-traveled rather than flown. Confused? Me too, and I lived it! But after so many trips, I'd become a seasoned pro at this whole "arriving when the rest of the world is fast asleep" thing.

Despite my body's protests—aching joints from being folded into a pretzel by my airplane seat and a level of sleep deprivation that bordered on the philosophical—I shuffled off the jetway and into the chaotic embrace of the arrivals terminal. All seemed normal. Grab a taxi, check into my hotel, and collapse face-first onto the nearest horizontal surface. Simple, right?

Wrong. Because, as the universe delights in reminding me, plans are merely suggestions. The moment I stepped outside, I was swallowed by a swirling sea of humanity: hands waving, feet shuffling, faces grinning, and luggage teetering in towers that defied every law of physics. Taxi drivers competed in an Olympic shouting match. Street vendors hawked snacks and trinkets I couldn't identify. Diesel engines coughed clouds of smoke into the already frenetic air. It was as if someone had cranked the volume on life to eleven.

For a split second, I wondered if I'd accidentally stepped into a Bollywood flash mob. But then, realization struck—like a strong cup of chai with a little too much ginger. It was Diwali, the grandest, loudest, most dazzling festival on the entire Indian subcontinent! Of course, the whole city was awake. Who needs sleep when you can have fireworks, feasts, and enough lights to give your retinas a standing ovation?

Fortunately, I was able to find a taxi that hadn't yet been commandeered, so hopping in, I was off to the Leela Hotel in Gurugram, a suburb of Delhi and near Cyber City, where all the tech companies congregate their employees. Arrival, check-in, unpack, shower; finally, at 3:30 AM, I was able to dive into bed.

The following day began for me at approximately 2:30 p.m. I had slept reasonably well, so I was hungry and headed downstairs to find the restaurant and once again partake of the marvelous breakfast buffet that the Leela offered to its guests. Before I even reached the restaurant, the hotel lobby greeted me with the distinctive aroma of air freshener desperately trying to mask the memory of hundreds of previous guests. Plush sofas dotted the lobby like little islands, each occupied by an assortment of travelers—an elderly couple debating the merits of their GPS app, a businessman furiously typing on his laptop, and a child methodically dismantling a decorative plant, one leaf at a time. In one corner, a tourist group huddled suspiciously around a guidebook, as if it contained top-secret blueprints.

When I finally arrived at the restaurant, I was disappointed but not surprised to discover that the breakfast buffet was no longer available for that day. Instead, I was handed a luncheon menu and seated at a table next to a window overlooking the street below and the pedestrian mall adjacent to the hotel.

As I perused the lunch menu, I was both delighted and baffled. Dishes with names longer than my shopping list beckoned from the page—Paneer Butter Masala, Chicken Chettinad, Baingan Bharta, and something mysteriously titled "Railway Mutton Curry." Every platter seemed to come with a side of rice, naan, or existential questions about how much spice one could handle. The dessert section was teased with Gulab Jamun and Kheer. However, my stomach insisted that 2:30 p.m. was still prime breakfast territory, so I bravely postponed exploring the culinary wonders of Indian cuisine...for now, opting instead for a pot of Americano coffee to begin righting myself.

I stirred the sugar cubes and the swirls of cream into the hot mixture promptly delivered to me while checking my email on my cell phone and reminding myself about the upcoming business agenda that would begin tomorrow morning. But for the remainder of this day, I was free to explore.

Since I hadn't yet accomplished my original goal of finding breakfast, I decided to head out of the hotel towards the pedestrian mall, which I had seen while seated in the hotel restaurant. As I ventured out of the hotel lobby, I was immediately assaulted by the hot, thick, smoky air that is all too common in the Delhi area. While not as severe in November as in other months of the year, it was still quite noticeable and served as a fresh reminder of the impact that 1.4 billion people and all that comes with it have on the environment in which they live.

The street in front of the hotel was much less crowded than it had been the day before at the airport. The weather was also more cooperative, and although it was hot, the air was drier and more comfortable. So, I began walking down the street towards the pedestrian mall, hoping to find something acceptable to pair with the coffee I carried with me in a paper to-go cup.

As I made my way down the back streets that fed visitors through the maze of shops, tiny eateries, clothing vendors, and jewelry stands, I noticed a sign in English that read, "Life is short — ride like a Sultan." Although I was far from royalty, the message piqued my interest. Historically, the Hindi royalty were known for collecting vintage English motor cars, particularly Rolls-Royce convertibles. I have always loved automobile sheet metal, and having never seen a vintage motorcar like this in person, I decided to take a look with some free time on my hands. With a sense of curiosity and no real expectations, I followed the sign into the alley, interested to see what I might find.

Much to my surprise, it was pretty dark inside. I could hear music playing softly in the background, and my sense of smell recognized a mixture of incense and something else, something natural; it was the straw on the floor beneath my feet. I barely had time to recenter my thoughts and senses when I saw her. She was as exquisitely beautiful as she was mysterious. I froze right where I had entered; my feet unable to move forward and introduce myself. My vision was fixated on her beautiful, large brown eyes, adorned with the longest of sweeping eyelashes. Bedroom eyes for sure.

I was standing there when I noticed her badge said "Suzie" in English, with some other characters underneath—probably Hindi. She looked right at me with her brown eyes, and I couldn't help but wonder if love at first sight, like you hear about in books, could happen in real life. What was I going to do? I was here on business, and my schedule was completely consuming. In twenty-four hours, I would be on my way to another stop in my return to India, a thousand miles from Delhi. But in this moment, nothing else seemed to matter.

As if Suzie could read my mind, she began to move towards me. My heart leaped; this was actually happening. Quickly, I began to wonder how best to greet her. She was wearing a badge written in both English and Hindi. What do I say? What should I do? How should I act? Do I respond to her advances? These questions ran through my mind like a fast-moving river anxious to reach the sea.

Life's surprises are often unpleasant, but if you dare to accept both the bad and the good, you can discover great joy and fulfillment. I had experienced enough of life's nasty surprises; maybe this time, my patience would bear fruit and bring me joy. The unpredictability of life is also a surprise. Just when you think that you have everything all figured out, boom!

Before our meeting could be realized, the significance and mystery of the moment were broken by the deafening sound of a fire alarm. In these crowded alleys, tiny shops, and dusty corners, a fire is a most unwelcome and hazardous event. So without a word, and any exchange of greetings, Suzie disappeared into chaos, and I ran for the light of the open air.

Sucking in the same smoky air, and winded from my abrupt dash from dark and fantasy to light and reality, I slowly walked back towards my hotel, a bit dazed, a little excited, and very disappointed. What of Suzie? Was that moment of connection a one-and-done? It was real, of that, I was sure.

Days later, returning home from my India adventure, I stared out of the airplane window, moving through the clouds one shattered dream at a time, traveling over the icy landscape of Greenland and past the muted eruptions of Iceland, I was making my way back to a more familiar reality once more. Why does life torture us this way? Why do you spend most of your life searching for 'something,' and when you finally realize what it is and have a chance to obtain it, you are left empty-handed?

Business needs change like the weather. Careers also move back and forth, up and down, presenting new opportunities, new friendships, and new experiences. I am well-accustomed to the whims of corporate fortune. I've always viewed change as an opportunity to build on the past and experience something new, adding more value to my next employer and giving me another skill to draw upon. In my new position, I had fewer opportunities to visit Mother India, although I still carried a healthy-sized file of friends and working associates who were still living there. And like old friends and coworkers, old memories run across the quiet moments of reflection.

But another business trip awaited! Now it was the Sonoran Desert that called to me. I was very familiar with this part of the country, having visited it on vacation or for business many times over the years. During those travel experiences, I had an opportunity to sample the beauty of the desert; the magic of the mesas lit up by the setting sun, the vast cosmos exposed in the desert night sky, and the silence that can only be found as the breath of God in the desert.

My business trip took me once again to Scottsdale and to the Camelback Resort. I had made friends with the tennis pro at the resort many years earlier, so whenever I traveled back to that area, I would send a note to my friend, and he always made sure that my accommodation there was comfortable and a bit less expensive.

As per my usual business travel schedule, I flew into Phoenix and made my way to Scottsdale, checking in at the resort and then finding one of my many favorite eateries in town. I decided to call my tennis pro friend and ask him to join me for dinner and to catch up over a few drinks in the desert starlight and sage. He was quick to accept the dinner invitation as his wife was suffering from a bug, and this was an opportunity for him to get out of the house. Our plan was launched.

We met at a favorite restaurant in Glendale, just outside of Phoenix. During our dinner conversation, my friend told me that he and his wife had tickets to the circus for that night, but she was ill and unable to go. So, he asked if I would be interested in going to the circus with him that night. Not having any specific plans for later that evening, I accepted his invitation.

Dinner behind us, we headed off in my rental car for Phoenix, a venue large enough to accommodate all that a circus brings to the table. After parking the car, we made our way to the entrance of the civic center, where the circus was. We went through the typical security checks, including metal detectors and a list of questions. Finally, we arrived at our seats, just a few rows from the main performance area. We grabbed a couple of beers and found our seats again just as the lights began to dim and the circus performers began to parade into the center ring.

The circus has never been my first choice for entertainment. Even as a child, I found the circus to be an odd mixture of skills and oddities offered up as entertainment. Quite frankly, I found the clowns to be terrifying! Laugh if you wish, but I always wondered if, after the circus was over, the clowns looked the way they did during the performance. No matter, it was a night out with a friend and in the Desert Southwest.

The performers made their way around the ring, waving to the crowd, followed closely by those aforementioned clowns. A bit of discomfort in me, perhaps, but I tried to focus on the other performers and give my lingering unsettledness a rest. The parade of performers and clowns made a full rotation around the main ring; it was now time for the animal acts to join the parade.

First came the dancing horses, all dressed appropriately. Following the horses were the chimpanzees, accompanied by their handlers. Next, Zebras; all moving slowly around the ring, acting quite spirited. Now it was time to parade the tigers, closely followed by the jugglers. Last of all, the finale: the parade of elephants.

Out came those marvelous pachyderms. Two by two, they started circling the ring with their riders seated royally atop. As the line of elephants drew closer to where we were sitting, I could read that each elephant wore a marker with its name printed on it.

As the elephants made their final turn closest to us, I spotted a familiar face—those same big, beautiful, brown eyes. The long curly eyelashes, it all looked so familiar. My mind struggled to connect my memories with the reality of that moment. Before I could solve on my own the mystery of my hidden memories, the last elephant in the parade passed by close enough for me to read the name on its marker – 'Suzie – Indian Elephant, New Delhi'

Each journey, each encounter, is a reminder: the world is vast, the heart is wild, and passion is always waiting just around the next corner, ready to turn the everyday into an adventure worth retelling.

Life is short – Ride an Elephant!

A Pathway Home

Poet Maya Angelou once wrote, "Life is not about the breaths you take, but about the moments that take your breath away."

That, to me, is the essence of finding passion in life's wrinkles, as we navigate the wormholes of our universe in search of a deeper meaning to our existence. It is an attempt to connect the pieces of our daily living into a strand of shiny memories, like pearls, that will adorn our lives and endure the scrutiny of our reflection and self-assessment. Each new dawn brings with it an opportunity to discover yet another tiny globe to sew on our string.

We breach the silence of each new day by giving thanks and praise to our Creator; then we become slaves to the daily routines that find their way into our lives with both subtle and profound impact. If we are not careful, over time, our routines become an integral part of our lives and, in many ways, help define us, or at the very least, paint a picture of how we wish to be perceived by others.

While life may provide us with the opportunity to jump from cloud to cloud as we move forward on our journey, it remains our responsibility to gather up all the lessons and experiences of our travels and to squeeze out a few drops of insight that can somehow improve our lives as well as the lives of those whom we meet along the way.

While our Creator's plan for each of us may include unequal amounts of opportunity and challenge, it is by our hand and determination, by our faith, and by living in humility and thanksgiving that we magnify our blessings in whatever form and quantity they may be. In so doing, we fulfill our purpose in living: to love one another and to give praise and glory to the one who left us here.

Woody Allen once said, "Eternity is a very long time… especially towards the end." If we strive to live in love with every moment of life and with all whom we share a destiny, then we need not wonder about the number of our days, but instead look forward to what awaits us both in this life and the next.

About the Author

Joseph M. Korzon grew up on State Street in New Haven, Connecticut. He has traveled extensively throughout his career, making friends and gaining experiences in India, the Philippines, Africa, Latin America, and across the United States. Both before and after his professional career, he has been actively involved with numerous charities, including the Juvenile Diabetes Research Foundation, the Connecticut Special Olympics, and other organizations focused on supporting individuals affected by traumatic brain injury and improving access to quality healthcare for all individuals.

He now resides in Ellington, Connecticut, where he is working on his latest collection of short stories and essays entitled *Shallow Waters—Our Search for Faith and Character in an Unwilling World*.

He has been recognized for excellence in journalism by the Connecticut Society of Professional Journalists and has been a regular contributor to *Connecticut Magazine*. He enjoys traveling, cycling, and spending time with family and friends, especially his two grandsons.

Website: joekorzonwhispers.com

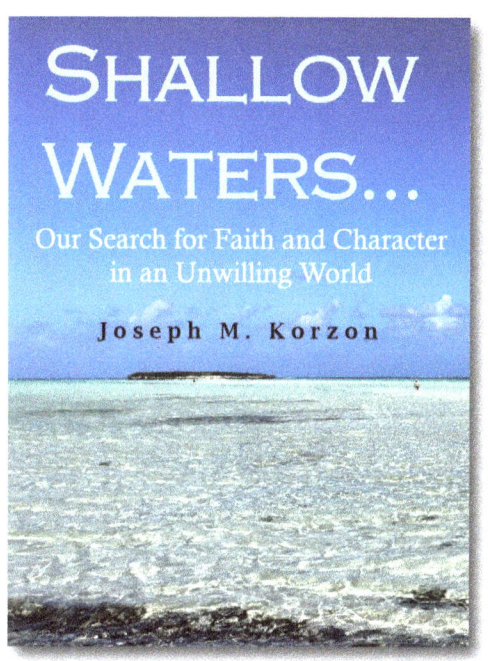

Coming Soon!

Shallow Waters:
Our Search for Faith and Character
in an Unwilling World

www.ingramcontent.com/pod-product-compliance
Lightning Source LLC
Chambersburg PA
CBHW061250230426
43664CB00024B/2907